Breaking
Out of
Plastic
Prison

Breaking Out of Plastic Prison

A 10-Step Program to Financial Freedom

James D. Dean
and Charles W. Morris

Foreword by Dan Allender
and Tremper Longman III

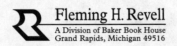

Fleming H. Revell
A Division of Baker Book House
Grand Rapids, Michigan 49516

© 1997 by James D. Dean

Published by Fleming H. Revell
a division of Baker Book House Company
P.O. Box 6287, Grand Rapids, MI 49516-6287

Printed in the United States of America

ISBN 1-56865-923-7

For current information about all releases from Baker Book House, visit our web site:
http://www.bakerbooks.com

To Jim Underwood, founder of Cornerstone and The Institute for Debt Free Living, mentor and best friend

Contents

Foreword

Do you struggle as we do?

Money matters can dissolve hope and joy. Money fears can devour a person's confidence and drain a couple of intimacy through accusation and blame. Love of money, though, is not the root of evil, it is the root of all evils.

As Christians concerned about what is really important, we don't want our minds lost in dreams of riches or weighed down with the fears of insufficient finances. Jesus said, "You cannot serve both God and money" (Matt. 6:24). We want to serve God, and him alone.

But we have to pay our bills. No matter how distasteful and emotionally sapping it seems to us, we must write the checks that pay for our food, shelter, education, books, insurance—the list seems to go on forever!

Jesus' words are so wise, because money can quickly become the thing that occupies our minds as we strategize how to get it and plan how to spend it. We find it hard sometimes not to worry and grow anxious about our daily needs and the desires of those close to us. In our modern society, very little is available unless we have the money for it, or even more dangerous, unless we have a credit card.

As our debt mounts and our children begin to attend college, our thoughts are increasingly captivated by the need to get more cash to pay it off. We may resist the temptation, but we find our minds and hearts overwhelmed by desire for money. Human beings, as Calvin so strikingly put it, are "idol factories," and though we may not think of it this way, money can quietly and quickly become our ultimate concern, an idol to which we are slaves. And even if we do not worship money, it is dreadfully easy to envy those who live above the constant grind because instead of working for their money, their money works for them (Ps. 73).

Dean and Morris understand the spiritual dimensions of this struggle, and that is what makes *Breaking Out of Plastic Prison* more than just another how-to financial book. Let us be quick to point out, though, that this book is very practical, giving us exceptionally helpful practical advice about how to get a hold of our finances, which so easily slip away from our control. As we read this extremely readable book, we both found help in dealing with our own financial situations, and for this we thank the authors.

However, as mentioned, we get more than practical advice. Dean and Morris rightly understand that "every economic decision has emotional and spiritual aspects." Using 1 Timothy 6:6–10 as a key text, they concretely demonstrate the danger of the "love of money." This perverse love does not have to be fueled by pure greed. Crushed by credit-card debt and just trying to make it for another day, Christians often allow the love of money to take on the force of necessity. When under this burden, it is hard to love the Lord our God, and him alone.

This book is not a Christian get-rich scheme. Too many Christian books these days make false claims concerning God's promises for prosperity in the present life. Others distort their reading of the Bible and demand that Christians live a simple lifestyle. Dean and Morris's book guards itself against these errors by being carefully scriptural throughout.

We strongly recommend this book to all Christians who struggle with finances, which we suspect is pretty nearly all Christians. It will not only help you struggle with your financial dilemmas, it will lead you to God himself.

Dan Allender
Tremper Longman III

1

How Did I Get Here?

I SAW MYSELF in the hopeless stares across the counseling desk. It happens frequently—seeing my reflection in the faces of men and women who have dug themselves into a financial pit of despair.

Today it was the dentist and his wife. Jim is twenty-eight. Jill twenty-seven. An outsider would think Dr. and Mrs. Dawson* had their lives together. Little would the outsider guess there were shouting, tears, and constant bickering in this two-year-old marriage, fatigued by $148,000 in education loans for a total of $172,000 owed to twenty-two creditors.

The outsider would see only a high income and professional prestige. Jim and Jill see a mountain of debt.

The Dawsons rent their home. They can't afford to buy and never hope to with a savings balance of only one thousand dollars. Granted, the rented seaside villa is opulent, even by Florida Gold Coast standards. A doctor must keep up his image, even if it means his wife also must work. "It costs more to live in Florida," they told me. Twenty long years remain just to pay off the dental school loans.

This young Christian couple arrived at our office caught in a grip of guilt that, if not checked, probably would lead them to break the marriage vows they had made to each other before God. Statistics show their marriage unlikely to survive the strain of a first or second

---

*Throughout this book, the names of people and the details of their stories have been changed to preserve their privacy.

child. Financial conflicts are the leading cause of today's astronomical divorce rate.

I am no psychologist. Nor am I a doctor. But the help I would give Jim and Jill would enable them to pour the missing financial foundation and rebuild their lives. I take special delight in seeing this happen again and again because it always brings back how it happened for me.

In 1978 my wife, Elizabeth, and I were in a similar state of hopelessness. I was a CPA, a fast-tracker at a Big Eight accounting firm. It seems like only yesterday we were newly married with hopes of making a high income and grabbing all the advantages my father never seemed to choose. Soon we saw those dreams slipping farther and farther away.

A STORY IN CONTRASTS

My friend, Jerry, and I started the same day at the international accounting firm of Ernst and Whinney. We were both right out of college. Shortly afterward I bought a Chevrolet Caprice Classic, only because I couldn't afford an Oldsmobile 98. It was in keeping with my position, I told Elizabeth. I needed the new car to fit my new successful role. Jerry chose to keep a rusting car, drivable but paid for. My Caprice Classic was paid for—by the bank, which I would be repaying for the next thirty-six months.

Jerry endured a lot of teasing for driving that jalopy, but three years later, when he left the firm to open a private practice with another CPA, he was debt-free and had saved a tidy sum.

On the other hand, three years later I had two new-car loans, a home mortgage, and my eye out for an even larger home as soon as my income began to rise. I envied Jerry going into business for himself, but there was no way I could follow his lead. My financial cushion was nonexistent.

Credit came easily. My wallet was tight with cards. MasterCard and Visa asked few questions of recent college grads joining the professional ranks. Department stores begged me to sign up for instant credit—only if we made a purchase, of course. Gasoline credit companies . . . well . . . I don't even think they bothered to check with a credit bureau. Higher credit limits for any card were an easy call away.

Fact:

Being a CPA doesn't mean you are good at handling your own money.

I kept my cars washed and waxed. We lived well, although never as well as we wished. But there were hints of a problem. Payday came only once a month even after I left Ernst and Whinney and went to higher paying jobs. We started having trouble reaching the end of the month with enough money. One day, I decided to get serious and take a personal survey of our spending. "Where should we cut back to remove the pressure?" I asked. Sound familiar?

My wife thought I had all the answers because of my education. So did I. The personal inventory seemed to show that our spending was reasonable. "We don't have a spending problem," I concluded, "we have an income problem."

Armed with this answer, I began searching for a solution.

A TALE OF EASY MONEY

A friend was willing to help. Jack came to my home and shared a business idea for making more money. I had respect for Jack's opinion because he was quite successful in his corporate career. The plan was to begin selling a high quality product in our spare time. By finding other friends to join the venture, I would make money from their sales and the sales of the friends they recruited. As my side business grew, I could then resign from what had become a dull accounting position. The part-time business would become full-time and never again would I struggle for more income. The money would flow. It sounded so promising. I thought I'd be able to retire at a young age.

The venture turned into many hours of extra work each week. Evening meetings became weekend meetings. Most everyone I met in the business was a Christian. By working just a little harder and a little more, I was assured, my dreams now plastered on our refrigerator door would most certainly come true.

The closet was filling up with motivational tapes and books. I frequently was attending weekend motivational rallies and having a lot of fun. However, my bank cards were "maxing out." For a while I didn't worry, convinced that the big payoff was just around the corner. But, after several years, I decided it was time for another personal inventory. We still couldn't make it through the end of the month. Our family of two had become three and the higher income never materialized. The reality: We were worse off than before we started building the side income.

Paydays were always a relief. The ritual involved driving to the bank during my lunch hour. "First of the month—why not go somewhere to eat?" I would tell myself, "You deserve it with such hard work." On the way home, with money in the bank, I would stop to get "just a few things we need." Over the next few days, Elizabeth and I would busy ourselves buying those "needed" items we had put off until payday. It was good to feel the financial strain eased. We usually decided the family deserved a night out—eating and doing fun things. "It's for the family," we would tell ourselves. Then, about the fifth of the month, I would take time to pay the bills and balance the

Fact: There are twenty-four hours in a day. Most Americans after sleeping, eating, commuting, and working have one to two hours per day of free time.

checkbook. There was never enough money to carry us to the end of the month. That meant another talk with Elizabeth and the agreement to scrimp until the next paycheck. Savings? What was that? Warning bells were sounding loudly, but I was deaf.

Then there was the unexpected that seemed to come around every other month. Maybe one of our cars would have a problem not covered under warranty. Or a home repair would come up we didn't anticipate. Often hundreds of dollars later—all on a credit card—we would be "fine."

The desire to own a business ran in my veins. But with no hope of that for the foreseeable future and my job more and more boring, I decided to look elsewhere. A friend suggested teaching. I had the credentials—education and work experience. So, we said good-bye to Nashville and moved to a small southern city where I had found a university faculty position. The friend on whose recommendation I had acted told me it would be easy—the hours were flexible and there was plenty of time to pursue other ventures.

After a year of teaching, the school offered a promotion. My appointment to direct a management development center on campus charged me with setting up seminars for the business community. The position brought prestige and a higher salary. Another child was on the way, so Elizabeth wasn't working. The higher income came in handy, but as I mixed more with the business community my desire grew for my own outside venture.

It's the American way to own your own business and I finally succumbed. That year, 1985, is etched in my memory. My hopes were high. I had tried so much and gained so little. Accounting was dull. Teaching didn't satisfy my longings to be my own boss. Running the management development center for the university had lost its appeal as my entrepreneurial spirit grew from seeing the success of others.

Procrastination is a failure to act, and I was about to act.

FOLLOWING A DREAM

I left the university to form a partnership with Miles, who had built a successful seminar business. Miles also had a steady income from his long-time work as a business consultant. People were flocking to his seminar, and we agreed I would handle the marketing side of the partnership. With hope that this was finally the right deal, I plunged into the venture. After a few months, seminar attendance was growing, but not enough to pay both salaries. With success in sight and my conviction that any new business needs up-front cash support, I used retirement money to pay living expenses. Months passed and success never came. We had no resources left to keep the business afloat. So, now renting our home, retirement funds gone, credit cards at their limit, and the bank account down to pennies, I bowed out, although not too gracefully.

I was in my thirties. Spiritually, I detected no problems. We went to church Sunday mornings and evenings. Our financial style looked normal and acceptable to me; our decisions reasonable if unsuccessful. Even when we couldn't pay all the bills, we gave a tithe off the top. All the time we struggled, I held onto the hope that God would bless me financially and fulfill my stubborn desire to be my own boss.

Finally the hope died. Worse off than I ever thought possible, we prayed for guidance. With no money, no savings, I did what more and more single and married people are forced to do—I rented a truck and became a prodigal son. With family and possessions in tow, I went back to my father and he took us in.

A job hunt ensued. We were shackled with thousands of dollars of debt. I was desperate for work. I breezed through dead-end jobs, my CPA training now useless. I hit bottom when I walked into the neighborhood 7-Eleven, swallowed hard, and asked the son of a high school friend for a job application. When I didn't hear anything, I called back and then called back again. The secretary at the district office told me I was overqualified and would never make clerk.

Like the father described by Jesus, my father must have realized I had learned some hard lessons and decided it was time for his offer of help. Having welcomed me home, he offered me a job in his successful architectural firm. We talked—but I wasn't looking for advice, and he lovingly allowed me to learn the hard way. We both decided this was temporary.

He also offered to pay off our large debts. But having seen me flounder as a habitual debtor, my father placed conditions on the money: it had to be repaid and it had to be paid with a fair rate of interest.

Fact: *Making minimum payments, it will take over fifteen years to repay a five-thousand-dollar balance on a credit card charging 18 percent interest. This glaring fact is not contained in the fine print of credit-card statements.*

As humbling as all this was, I knew God was at work in my life. Hard lessons were being taught and, as with anyone caught in a deeply rooted sin pattern, deep changes were required. Such changes rarely occur overnight, but with divine leading, they do come.

My thirst for financial success had been denied. Suddenly I was thirsty for the Lord, his Word, and, of course, his leading. For the first time in ten years, I felt peace.

The job my father gave me was not high paying. But it was enough. We had a roof, food, and a single loan payment toward becoming debt-free. The interest rate was reasonable, unlike charge-card rates more than twice the amount.

The healing process had begun. My desire for freedom from my pattern of using debt to bail myself out led to much time in the Bible and on my knees, asking God to teach me exactly where I had strayed.

What a few months earlier I would have considered a tedious, unproductive road, now became something like a holy quest. My intensive study of God's Word yielded ten lessons—about myself and about money. These lessons have served me—and those who come to me for help—again and again.

2

Living a Double Life

HUMBLED. Here I was, after all my lofty dreams, under my father's roof, paying off debts while working for low wages, and actually being thankful for food and shelter. All my "can do" self-confidence was squelched.

Yet, as painful as it might be, this newfound humility was like a searchlight shining on God's Word. Verses that used to roll off me were coming home to my heart with a flash of brilliance.

God began showing me that when my heart is set on acquiring material things like new cars and bigger houses—no matter what the cost—I am actually falling "into temptation and a trap" that could plunge me "into ruin and destruction" as it says in 1 Timothy 6:9. I had considered my life committed to Christ. I attended church, tithed, and did a lot of the right Christian things, but in reality the love of money was my first priority.

The words of 1 Timothy 6:6–10 began to speak directly to my heart, and for the first time I could understand God's warning about my life:

> Godliness with contentment is great gain. For we brought nothing into the world, and we can take nothing out of it. But if we have food and clothing, we will be content with that. People who want to get rich fall into temptation and a trap and into many foolish and harmful desires that plunge men into ruin and destruction. For the love

of money is a root of all kinds of evil. Some people, eager for money, have wandered from the faith and pierced themselves with many griefs.

Of course, I hadn't realized I was living this way. I thought I had my priorities straight. But a good friend opened my eyes to what I was really pursuing in life. He pointed out that my desire for material success was actually an idol.

I didn't follow what he meant at first. I thought of idols as being those objects created and worshiped by pagans in the Old Testament. Then he explained that an idol is anything we desire and seek ahead of God. It can be success, health, careers—anything in the world.

The gentle apostle John has some strong words on this subject:

> Do not love the world or anything in the world. If anyone loves the world, the love of the Father is not in him. For everything in the world—the cravings of sinful man, the lust of his eyes and the boasting of what he has and does—comes not from the Father but from the world.
>
> 1 John 2:15–16

Then John further encourages us to keep our priorities straight by adding in verse 17, "The world and its desires pass away, but the man who does the will of God lives forever." I had never before grasped the significance of what John is saying in these verses. He is describing the "world" as a sort of system based on the principles of craving and boasting. We want things. In these verses, the objects of our cravings are not sexual, they are material. Like a new car or a bigger house. And—get this—we want them not only for our pleasure, but to satisfy our egos and to feed our pride.

My self-worth was tied up in what I drove and where I lived, not in Jesus Christ.

YOU CAN'T SERVE TWO MASTERS

Now that I was experiencing the mandatory humility of hitting bottom financially, I could see that pride had been fueling my drive

> **Fact:** Jesus tells us we cannot serve two masters. It is impossible because we will always love one and hate the other. We cannot live a double life.

for success and my dislike for driving older cars and living in a smaller house. In the world, prosperity elevates us and material possessions give us status. I had unconsciously bought into this perspective.

God calls this idolatry. Jesus tells us in Matthew 6:24 we cannot serve two masters. It is impossible because we will always love one and hate the other. We cannot live a double life.

Because of my strong desire for the finer things of life, I always struggled with this passage. It seemed to be saying that a desire for something nicer than the utilitarian provision of our needs was going against God. I now believe it's talking about the things that capture our hearts. Do we desire material possessions more than our Lord and his kingdom? If we make the Lord Jesus Christ our joy and our delight, we won't hold too tightly to other things or worry too much if we lose them. And after we die they won't matter anyway.

The difficulty is that we live in a world that compels us to possess more and more, to find our identity in what we possess, and to feel deeply deprived, even humiliated, if we don't have what we want. The whole thrust of advertising is to make us feel we cannot live without what's being sold, so we will go out and buy it. It is awesome to realize that, according to Isaiah 2:19–21, when God stands in judgment against the proud and arrogant, they will cast their idols to the "rodents and bats" as they flee in terror. I remembered all the times I had wrestled with God, praying for him to give me all my worldly desires. I had been living a double life, and God was bringing me to repentance.

The Lord was showing me that there are two contrasting king-doms—his kingdom and the kingdom of the world. We can't live with one foot in each kingdom because they have opposing motives and opposing goals. He calls us to "flee from all this [the desire to be rich], and pursue righteousness, godliness, faith, love, endurance and gentleness" (1 Tim. 6:11).

We can easily get tangled in questions about what God wants in the area of material things. How much do I keep? How much do I give away? How big a house is too big? Should I take the vacation when there are people in desperate need around the world? My fam-ily has been living in a town home for the last eight years, but we would like to own a single family home with a garage. Because other things are a higher priority, such as a Christian school for our chil-dren and my wife, Elizabeth, not working outside the home, we have not been able to buy the home we want, but the desire is still there. Is this wrong?

I don't think these questions have answers. Rather, we will find that as we repent of our idolatry and ask God to expose our double hearts, he will free us from the grip of our desires. The Lord will become our delight. He will create in us a love for his kingdom above anything else. Then we will be free—to enjoy the good things he gives with thankfulness, to do without them, or even to give them away with great joy.

THE WORLD'S VIEW VERSUS GOD'S VIEW

What we need is to have our thinking shaped by the Word and the Spirit, not by the world. Here are four viewpoints on possessions that characterize the world's perspective contrasted with God's point of view. I believe the Lord is telling us to plant both feet squarely in his kingdom and to turn back whenever we find ourselves drifting into the world's perspective.

Self-Worth

World's view: Possessions and accomplishments make the man. The wealthy man is treated as though he has more value than the poor man. Doors open for him and he receives honor that a poor man never gets. Even in the church this attitude creeps in and rich men find themselves more often on boards and appointed to leadership positions. When I buy into this perspective, it affects the way I treat people and how I define myself. I automatically slot myself into the world's hierarchy, while I struggle for a higher slot. When I'm driving up to a nice restaurant in my new car, I feel on top of the world. I have status. When I am driving a clunker, I feel a little ashamed. I am finding my identity in what I own.

God's view: "Be on your guard against all kinds of greed; a man's life does not consist in the abundance of his possessions" (Luke 12:15). These are Jesus' own words. God does not place any more value on the rich man than he does the poor man. Jesus had nowhere to lay his head and, in fact, usually could be found among the poor. Yet, he was at home in the rich man's house and, to the chagrin of his disciples, refused to give the rich and important any special honor. God is impartial, and he tells us to be the same. The Book of James warns us not to give special treatment to people with more possessions but to love each person as we love ourselves. Of course, we can't divide the world into just two categories of rich and poor. Most of us see ourselves as somewhere in the middle. It is the attitude that "the higher we are up the scale the more value we have" that God hates. Man's possessions and accomplishments are nothing in his sight. To God, all the glory of man is like a flower that springs up and then fades away, and he is calling us to look at things the way he does. That means being on guard against ladder-climbing.

Ownership

World's view: What's mine is mine. The world is naturally possessive. We calculate what we have in the bank, the value of our possessions, the size of our house, and we consider all this as our rightful property. After all, we earned it, didn't we? Through our own hard work, or superior planning, or maybe an inheritance from our families, these things have come to us. Usually we aren't satisfied with our personal hoard. We cast our eyes on our neighbor's things and sometimes wish they were ours. I see my own possessiveness coming out in the way I act toward my cars, especially a new car. I spend a lot of time making sure it is maintained and cleaned and waxed. It is very difficult for me to loan my car to someone. If I come out to the parking lot and find a scratch, I am outraged.

God's view: "The earth is the LORD's, and everything in it, the world, and all who live in it" (Ps. 24:1). The realization that I don't really own anything, but that God has ultimate ownership of everything has helped break my grip on possessions. He has control over them and he gives them and he takes them away. In his sovereignty, he can cause our plans to succeed or fail, and all our efforts to do business and make money will come to nothing unless God wills them (James 4:13–17). As an accountant and businessman, I had learned that successful people are independent-minded and take control of their circumstances. I believed that good planning and determination would take me to my goals. I was determined not to give up until I reached my objective. I planned my strategy, tried to take into account all the contingencies, and went after predictable results. There was only one problem. Life is not predictable. I am not in control; God is. As 1 Samuel 2:6–7 says: "The LORD brings death and makes alive; he brings down to the grave and raises up. The LORD sends poverty and wealth; he humbles and he exalts." This means the things I possess are really gifts from him and I have no right to them. He doesn't want me to grab them and run. He wants me to hold them loosely and be willing to share, willing to let go if necessary. The bottom line is that I don't even have a right to myself. Christ has purchased me, and at what a price! I belong to him. I am part of his special, holy inheritance, and as I surrender to his lordship he fills my heart with his love. Material possessions naturally lose their attraction. People calling Christ their master can honestly say "So what?" to the bigger house and the new car.

Security

World's view: Security logically comes from a fat financial cushion. Life is full of uncertainty. We need a safety net in the form of assets to catch us if we fall. Our net worth is our protection against bankruptcy, or homelessness, or any other terrifying financial catastrophes that can come to us. If we don't watch out for our interests, who will?

God's view: "Do not worry about your life, what you will eat or drink; or about your body, what you will wear . . . your heavenly Father knows that you need them" (Matt. 6:25, 32b). According to the Bible, being worried over providing for ourselves will so weigh us down and preoccupy us that the day Christ returns will catch us like a thief. In the same way a big stockpile of material resources will create the illusion of immortality and blind us to the need to prepare for eternity. Jesus gives us the antidote for both of these attitudes in Matthew:

> "Do not store up for yourselves treasures on earth, where moth and rust destroy, and where thieves break in and steal. But store up for yourselves treasures in heaven, where moth and rust do not destroy, and where thieves do not break in and steal. For where your treasure is, there your heart will be also . . . No one can serve two masters. Either he will hate the one and love the other or be devoted to the one and despise the other. You cannot serve both God and Money.
>
> "Therefore I tell you, do not worry about your life, what you will eat or drink; or about your body, what you will wear . . . Who of you by worrying can add a single hour to his life? . . . So do not worry, saying, 'What shall we eat?' or 'What shall we drink?' or 'What shall we wear?' For the pagans run after all these things, and your heavenly Father knows that you need them. But seek first his kingdom and his righteousness, and all these things will be given to you as well."
>
> Matthew 6:19–21, 24–33

Jesus commands some radical departures from the way the world thinks in these verses. First, he says that possessions are not permanent. Ultimately they only belong to us for the span of our earthly years. The things that happen to us in this life, our gains and our losses, what we have or don't have, are far outweighed by our eternal destiny. Possessions aren't worth the importance we place on them—neither the worry nor the false security they give us.

Second, Jesus says that running after security as the world does is fruitless. We can't really achieve any kind of security. We can't even add a day to our lives. When we are called to appear before God, our stockpiles and barns full of security will count for nothing.

Third, according to Jesus' word, our heavenly Father will provide for us. He is our ultimate security. He knows we need clothes and food, and we can trust him for these things.

Fourth, Jesus says that this promise of provision gives us the security to pursue God's kingdom. We don't have to live fearfully, pursuing our own interests. In fact, we can't live both ways. Here is that double life again. We can only serve one master.

Contentment

World's view: My contentment lies in meeting my family's needs first and then getting our "wants." We pay the bills and hope to have a little left over so we can enjoy life a bit. All of us have our wants. A new dress when everything in the closet is all too familiar, a gadget for our camcorder, travel, eating out, the old couch recovered . . . the list of things we would buy if we had the money is endless. The high-tech world of computers has added a whole new dimension to many of our lives . . . and to the list of things we can't live without: the new version of our favorite software, the fastest chip, the highest resolution monitor . . . and on it goes. If we get a windfall or a raise, the increase is sucked into the vacuum of our desires. A recent article on lottery winners was revealing. After paying off debts and buying a new house, most people indulged in luxuries they never thought they would be able to afford: leather coats, diamond rings, exotic trips. This seems normal from the world's point of view. What would you do if you won the lottery or inherited $10 million?

God's view: "Godliness with contentment is great gain" (1 Tim. 6:6). Please don't misunderstand me. God gives us good things. He created the earth full of wonderful things for us to enjoy, and I don't think he delights in meaningless self-sacrifice. We can receive his blessings with thanksgiving. But there is a contentment that comes from receiving the simple pleasures God gives us without actively pursuing them. As Christians we cannot continue to live for indulgence and pleasure. We have been called to please the One who died for us. This is our freedom and our joy.

So how can we find this contentment and break the stranglehold of our desires? I used to think contentment was a depressing word. I thought it meant being satisfied with the way things are because

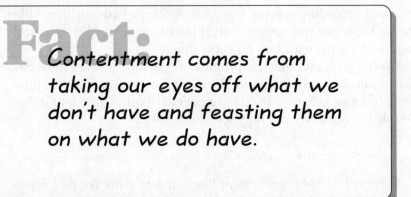

Fact: *Contentment comes from taking our eyes off what we don't have and feasting them on what we do have.*

they probably aren't going to get any better. But contentment is a much more dynamic concept.

Christian contentment comes from taking our eyes off what we don't have and feasting them on what we do have. Think about the love of Christ for you. Let your new identity in Christ sink in. You are God's child. He has been pleased to give you his kingdom. Are you frustrated by all the time it will take to pay off your debts? Spend time meditating on the fact that Jesus has paid the big debt for you. Do you really get upset that you can't buy a house with one more bedroom so your kids don't have to share a room? Let the heavenly mansion Jesus has promised become more real in your life. Does it look like car repairs will replace your vacation this year? Delight yourself in the Lord. And develop the habit of being thankful for the blessings you enjoy—the beautiful world God has created, your loved ones, your freedom, your health. If you practice this kind of thinking, your heart will be changed. Get into the habit of saying "So what?" to the things you cannot have, because of the greatness of the riches you have in Christ.

As you go through this book and implement the suggestions for getting your finances under control, you will be faced with saying "no" or "later" to many of your desires. You may find that the plan of action you come up with will take longer than you thought. The greatest safeguard against giving up is joy and contentment in the Lord. Believe me, I know, and I have to remind myself every day.

STEWARDSHIP

If you have been a Christian for any time at all, you have heard the word *stewardship*. Churches have stewardship drives to raise money for new buildings or to obtain weekly pledges. Before I became a committed Christian, the annual stewardship sermon was never one of my favorites. I always felt guilty for not giving more. Stewardship is not a term we use in everyday life, and it has been misused even in Christian circles.

So what does stewardship really mean? The *Random House Unabridged Dictionary* defines stewardship as managing another's property. The implication for Christians is that everything in this world belongs to God and he has given each of us possessions to manage.

A manager must always be responsive to what the owner wants done with the assets, or risk being fired. As stewards managing God's resources, we must be tuned in to his concerns and his purposes.

We're not truly free to spend or consume what we possess without concern for our accountability to God. As Ron Blue put it in his book *Master Your Money*, "every spending decision is a spiritual decision." When we stand before God in heaven, we will be asked to account for how we managed his possessions (2 Cor. 5:9–10). What would be the effect if you thought about that day of accountability with every decision you made?

The biblical idea of stewardship goes back to Joseph, who was Pharaoh's steward and managed all the resources of Egypt. Because of the wisdom he received from God, Joseph was able to save the Egyptians from seven years of famine and preserve the people of God from extinction (Genesis 41–47).

In a parable of stewardship, Jesus asks: "Who then is the faithful and wise servant, whom the master has put in charge of the servants in his household to give them their food at the proper time? It will be good for that servant whose master finds him doing so when he returns. I tell you the truth, he will put him in charge of all his possessions" (Matt. 24:45–47).

Paul reminds the Corinthians he was entrusted (as a steward) with "secret things" by God, that is, things that could not be discovered through human wisdom but could only be revealed by God (1 Cor. 4:1–2). As such, he is compelled to share the gospel.

Peter says we must use all the gifts God has given us, faithfully administering (or "stewarding") God's grace in its various forms. He includes hospitality, speaking, and serving (1 Peter 4:9–12).

As I studied this idea of stewardship, I understood for the first time what it is all about. I was wasting "my" resources on poor financial decisions and spending money on myself for things that were not that important. I was paying high interest rates on credit-card debt incurred to satisfy my desires. But God has great patience when he deals with us. If we set out to bring our financial lives under control and manage our money for the causes of his kingdom because we want to please him in every way, then we can be assured that he will be pleased with every little step we take. You see, we are not only stewards, but sons and heirs with Christ. He is not only holding us accountable as managers but calling us into the joy of partnership for his purposes. So we live with a solemn obligation and a wonderful privilege.

I will never forget Susan and Daniel coming to Cornerstone. I knew them and it was obvious they deeply loved the Lord. A year before they came to me, they sensed his calling to the mission field. Prayer and asking for the wisdom of other believers seemed to confirm the call. They applied to a mission agency and received preliminary approval. When they came to Cornerstone, they had just received a heavy blow. They had been turned down. The reason? Their finances weren't in order. They had too much debt. Their call to the mission field was placed on hold.

I have counseled many faithful believers who were serving the Lord full time but almost lost their ministry because of financial problems and debt from indulgent spending.

Being responsible with our finances is like having our lamps in readiness for the Lord's call. For that reason, I believe managing debt wisely (ideally being debt-free) and developing the habit of living on a budget—while saving for future needs—is a vital part of our obedience as Christians. As you read the remaining chapters, I hope you will keep returning to these ideas. They will encourage you to persevere.

ACTION
STEP 1:

Find Your
Current
Financial
Condition

3
- - - - - - - - - -
Reality Check

LIKE MY FATHER, I love to read maps. As a small boy, before taking trips, I would pore over the gas station maps, plotting ways to get from point *A* to point *B*. I learned a valuable lesson preparing for those vacations—before you start, you plan, and every good plan has three parts:

Part 1: Know where you are.
Part 2: Know where you want to go.
Part 3: Know the route to get there.

My training as a CPA taught me that planning applies to finance. If someone had asked me twelve years ago what to do and in what order, my accountant's brain could immediately have rattled off a course of action, step by step. But while I had the "head" knowledge, the rest of me resisted. The Lord had to take me to no job and the depths of having a bank account balance of only ten dollars and outstanding bills amounting to over ten thousand dollars.

This book will show you how to develop a plan. But that won't break your resistance. No system will bring about deep change. I truly believe the first step on the road to freedom is asking the Lord to show you what needs to change. We can be blind to our patterns of sin. Only his power and grace will allow us to see and overcome a lifetime of bad habits.

I recall a woman coming to my office, sitting down in the chair across from my desk, and saying, "I cannot change." She meant it! She believed there was no hope. Yet, as I shared from my experience and that of others, a glimmer of hope began to appear. She began to trust in God and gained the courage to try again, in dependence on him.

The greatest example of change is Christian rebirth. God reaches down in his mercy, cleanses our sinful hearts, and breathes new life into our souls. We are deeply changed. The same power that raised Jesus from the dead is now at work within us, capable of performing the relatively minor miracle of changing our money habits.

I don't just believe this can happen. I know it. My wife, Elizabeth, and I saw it take place in our lives. We could never have changed on our own, individually or as a couple.

If you have problems, I would challenge you to pause at this point in the book and take your problems to the Lord in prayer. Stop blaming others. Accept responsibility for your plight but then ask God to take over. If you are married, I ask you to do what might seem the impossible—go to your spouse and together pray for God's help now.

FOUR FINANCIAL PERSONALITY STYLES

One of the first things God did to change my financial habits was to give me insight into my personality. Certain types of people are

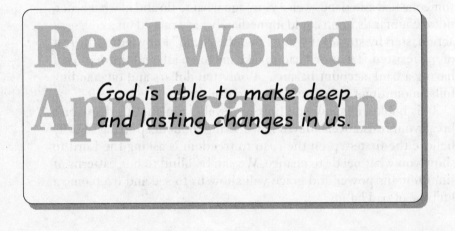

Real World Application:

God is able to make deep and lasting changes in us.

more likely to have money problems than others. The self-disciplined, methodical type seems to have fewer problems handling money than the more outgoing, carefree person who finds it easy to throw caution to the wind. Some people have trouble taking responsibility for their problems. They blame-shift and deny and use any strategy to avoid facing the situation squarely, because the fear is too great. Others periodically struggle to overcome, but they quickly give up, going back to their old ways because they see so little hope.

In 1994 the Public Agenda Foundation conducted a study on retirement planning. This nonprofit research and education group discovered that an alarming number of people underestimate their retirement needs. Interviewing nonretired leaders in government, media, and business, the New York City think tank found that 70 percent of those interviewed said they will be worse off financially than the current retired generation. Of those surveyed, one-third had saved practically nothing for their retirement years.

What was the problem? According to Agenda researchers, it was personality style. The survey identified four financial personality profiles that affect the way people handle their money. You may be a combination of all four at different times and in different circumstances, or you may consistently fit into only one.

Impulsives are free-spenders who have trouble denying themselves. They tend to live in the present and worry little about the future. They act impulsively and resist restraints. They don't think twice about increasing debt levels.

Strugglers are fearful and feel that things are out of their control. They feel overwhelmed by the financial demands of the moment and cannot see any light at the end of the tunnel. They use credit cards (debt) when they see no other way, which is most of the time.

Deniers refuse to worry. They tend to be blindly optimistic and believe that someone or something will come to their rescue. They overestimate their assets and underestimate their needs and they avoid the reality of their debt.

Planners know exactly what their goals are. They have a clear anticipation of their future. They know where they spend their money. They make decisions beforehand about what they will buy and what they will save and they stick with them. They use debt cautiously, if at all.

I began to see that I was basically an ineffective struggler without a plan—someone who tended to try quick fixes and, when they didn't work, give up in despair. I would then console myself that I had tried. I blamed the government, the economy, my employer, or my lack of employment for putting me in this impossible situation where there was too little money and too many financial demands. I needed to change my style.

Whether you're a struggler like I was, or an impulsive or a denier, you need to act like a planner. And that means you need a plan. Does that overwhelm you? Does it make you want to throw away this book and forget it? Do you think it's impossible?

Let me tell you—if I could do it, so can you. God will make the changes. You can take control of your finances and begin to live a life of financial freedom. Don't use your personality style as an excuse. I've run into many people who tell me they're just not the accountant type. Some have prided themselves on their carefree ways, on not being uptight about things. But when financial realities reach the crisis stage, these excuses offer little consolation.

I have finally become a planner. One of the first keys to changing my financial personality was to take responsibility for our finances and quit blaming circumstances. The second key was clarifying my

Real World Application:

According to God's Word, we should all be planners.

objectives. The third key was learning about and applying the techniques needed to accomplish my objectives.

Changing my behavior was not easy. I did it in increments over time. For example, I began thinking about how to save money every time I spent. Then I began to think about whether I could do without a purchase altogether, or at least postpone it.

According to God's Word, we should all be planners. Proverbs 14:8 says, "The wise man looks ahead. The fool attempts to fool himself and won't face facts" (LB).

Planners look at the map before taking a trip. They find out where they are. They decide where they need to be. They choose a route and they determine how long it will take. It's simply a matter of taking one step after another. With every step it gets easier.

The first step is to know where you are . . . now!

MEET THE ROBINSONS

Mark and Paula Robinson were like many couples I've counseled. They were not planners. Both age thirty-five, married twelve years, with two great kids, the Robinsons were a Christian couple with many blessings. Mark had a secure job as an engineer with a large company that paid a moderate income with good benefits. Paula worked part time as an administrative assistant for their church. Their children, Rhonda, age ten, and Carl, age seven, were doing well in Christian school. Life should have been good. Yet when they came to my office, they were unhappy with each other and feeling stressed by money worries.

Mark tended to be impulsive. He worked hard all day and when the day ended, he wanted a reward. Dinner out, a movie, a new tie— little rewards, but they added up. He bought the pop-up camper on the spur of the moment at a recreational vehicle show.

Paula was more of a denier. She figured Mark knew what he was doing, and she didn't want to think about money anyway. The few times she handled the family checkbook, bills often weren't paid on time, and the statement was never opened to find a balance.

Meanwhile, they had some debts to pay off, including a student loan that never seemed to go away from Mark's night classes toward an advanced degree he needed to be promoted. The Robinsons had paid off one car but owed quite a bit on another car, the camper, and a couple of credit cards.

The crisis came when Paula realized Mark had been dipping into their savings to pay the bills each month. A check bounced, and Mark had to admit there was no money left in savings to cover it.

So what did the Robinsons and I do? We talked about personality styles and how they get us into financial trouble. As we discussed Mark's impulsiveness and Paula's denial, the blame shifting began to lessen between them. Then we looked at God's Word and talked about how to become planners.

Mark was especially convicted by Proverbs 27:23–24: "Be sure you know the condition of your flocks, give careful attention to your herds; for riches do not endure forever, and a crown is not secure for all generations."

As Mark put it, "My riches have been disappearing pretty quickly; I'm worried the family 'crown' won't be there to pass on to my children. I can't see how I can so much as help pay their college tuition the way my dad helped me."

Proverbs 27:23–24 was the theme verse the Robinsons adopted as they put together the first part of their financial plan: Know where you are. To know where you are, you just have to answer two questions: What do we own? What do we owe?

What do we own?

What accountants call assets are simply the things we possess— the twentieth-century version of our herds and flocks. We need to

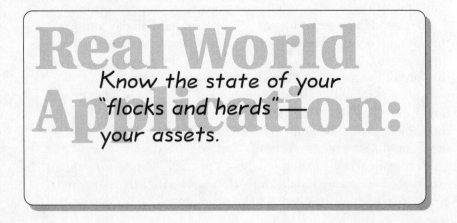

Real World Application:

Know the state of your "flocks and herds"— your assets.

put dollar amounts on them based on their present market value or, in other words, what we could sell them for. The idea of coming up with a list of personal assets was a little intimidating to Paula. We did it quickly without getting bogged down with precise amounts.

Look over the Robinsons' list of assets on their personal financial statement in figure 1 in appendix A. They have some cash on hand but it will be going out quickly to pay bills and buy necessities. Their home was ten years old when they bought it three years back, so the kitchen appliances and air conditioner probably will need replacing in the next two years. They also have their cars, furniture, jewelry, and camper and a little bit set aside for retirement.

Now, turn to the blank Personal Financial Statement (fig. 11 in appendix A) and do what the Robinsons did. Quickly, using estimates, write down what you own. (Use a pencil.)

What do we owe?

What accountants call liabilities are simply the amounts of money we currently owe. To find that figure, we estimate how much we would have to pay if we wrote a check today and paid off everything. The Robinsons didn't get bogged down calling around to find out their exact payoff balances. To save time and stress, they simply filled in estimates.

Look over the Robinsons' list of debts in figure 1. They have bills of $800. Their home mortgage is $95,000. The educational loan is $4,000. They owe $7,800 on one of their cars and they still have $4,400 of credit-card debt.

Now, turn back to figure 11 and quickly list your debts.

Add up your assets and add up your liabilities. Subtract and you have your net worth. In other words, you know where you are. Don't be discouraged if your net worth is less than the Robinsons' or even a negative amount. No matter how far you are from your goal, at least you know where you are and you can start planning how to improve. The first time Elizabeth and I completed this exercise, we had a negative net worth.

SETTING YOUR GOALS

The Robinsons weren't in as bad shape as they thought they were. They didn't have a lot of debt for a middle-income family. But they didn't have many assets either. If they had a real emergency—if Mark lost his job, for instance—they probably would have to cash in their retirement funds to get by.

In the chapters that follow, we'll explore goal setting. I've had to realize that my own finances are limited and I can't always accomplish every goal as quickly as I would like. It's important to put your goals in order of priority, and that means making choices.

The Robinsons had two major goals. They wanted out of debt and they wanted to start saving for their children's college education. They spent a few minutes looking at their latest credit card bills and then filling out the List of Debts form (fig. 2 in appendix A) so they would know exactly where they were in terms of their debt. I assume that for anyone reading this book, getting out of debt is a high priority goal. If that is true for you, take the time to get started now.

Turn to figure 12 in appendix A and write down your own list of debts.

In the next chapter we'll look at how to set up a budget that really works. It's the first step in part three of planning a trip: Once you know where you want to be, find the route to get there.

4

Feast and Famine

JENNIFER OGDEN thought her life was going along nicely. A happy marriage, upscale home, and two lovely children. She had it all, until one day her husband, Jerry, didn't come home. In fact, he never came home again, and the only word she received was the notice when he filed for divorce.

You can imagine that her world was shattered. Thad and Rachael were under age ten and couldn't understand why Daddy didn't come home from work anymore. It was even more confusing for them to have their dad's former secretary as a second mother.

Jennifer had been out of the workplace since she married ten years before. Her life had been spent working hard as a wife and mother. Her soon to become "ex" earned an upper-middle-class salary, but he was determined to fight against paying alimony and tried to ward off what he described as excess child support.

She couldn't believe it. Where was the man she had known and loved since they both graduated from college?

Having never balanced the checkbook—much less worried about how to make ends meet—Jennifer started reading the classifieds. How was she going to put food on the table? How would she pay for an attorney? What would they do for Christmas three weeks away? These questions kept her awake at night, and Jerry wasn't offering any help.

Their church was no refuge for her. Jerry started going to a new church, but Jennifer kept going to the old church because of her children's friends. She tried to understand the couples who had been best friends as they greeted her politely but remotely. Even in the eyes of the pastor, she thought she could detect questions about where to place the blame.

When she arrived for our first meeting, Jennifer had never felt so alone in her life. She liked people, needed people, and suddenly there seemed nowhere to go. The Cornerstone visit proved a turning point. We couldn't help solve the marriage problems; Jerry was quite happy in his new arrangement and found a church willing to accept him and his new wife. But we could help Jennifer survive what overnight had become a cruel world. We proceeded immediately to determine what she owed and her monthly expenses. For someone who had never kept a checkbook, she had a remarkable memory for monthly expenses.

Although Jennifer had always been ready to spend, the emotional shock and uncertainty were enough for her to readily accept the principle of establishing a budget. She could see that tracking her spending and keeping a budget would

1. allow her to become more aware of where she was spending money, which would reduce impulsive purchases and increase her ability to shop wisely.
2. provide freedom from worry about finances since boundaries would be set.
3. offer the discipline to control spending on lower priority items, leaving more money for higher priorities.
4. open communication with a spouse, if she remarried, about financial matters before critical problems developed.

Some clients have difficulty accepting the Scripture, "The wise man looks ahead. The fool attempts to fool himself and won't face facts" (Prov. 14:18 LB). Jennifer was no fool, and for the first time she was looking ahead. Her sessions with Cornerstone took on new meaning as she began to realize she was not alone. She took heart in our Lord's words, "I will never leave you."

By the third session, the panic attacks had lessened. Through analyzing what she had and what she owed and setting up a budget, she could make some concrete decisions. Life was no longer out of control.

First, we looked at her assets. Jerry had agreed to leave her the house, as long as she would make the mortgage payment. The house was purchased shortly after she and Jerry were married and was in a fast growth area where houses were in great demand. The value of the four-bedroom, three-bath house with a swimming pool had skyrocketed to $250,000 with an equity of $150,000.

The solution for Jennifer was plain. The house went on the market and sold for cash within a month. After closing, Jennifer found herself with $140,000 profit, ready to invest. We helped her choose a safe place for her newfound gain, which returned 6 percent interest.

Now she needed a place to live. Thad and Rachael were excited about moving. It didn't matter to them that the "new" house was a rental. One week later, she found a three-bedroom, one-bath home still close to church and friends. The house came with no garage (which she didn't need in a southern climate) but had a large, fenced back yard, perfect for the family's basset hound. The rent was six hundred dollars, just what she needed.

The last piece of the puzzle came a few days later in response to her resumes and job interviews. A medical clinic called to say it couldn't offer a full-time job, but would she be interested in a part-time job from 9:00 A.M. to 2:00 P.M. each day? She hadn't known it when she applied for full-time work, but this was exactly what she needed now to be with the kids before and after school, while at the same time helping meet her budget.

Hopelessness had turned to hope, and for that Jennifer and the children thanked the Lord. All along, Jennifer had put her needs in the Lord's hands. She and the children prayed every day and took hold of the Lord's promises to provide food and shelter for his children. God knew her needs and provided for them.

The budget was a practical key to ending Jennifer's initial panic. It allowed her to make calm decisions with sound judgment. While nothing more than a realistic plan for spending, a budget can put life back on a steady track and take away a lot of uncertainty and stress.

Budget Basics

For years, I had been hearing about the benefits of keeping a budget, and I didn't want to do it. Running through my mind were thoughts like: "I don't have much time. It's too much work. A budget would make me feel too restricted and too controlled." I also had this image of someone who lived on a budget as a conservative, boring person who was obsessed with money and couldn't spend a dime without making a major issue out of it.

At the risk of sounding like the host of a late-night infomercial, the technique I'm proposing will make all the difference. I don't have to spend hours each week working with my budget, yet it has helped me feel more in control of my spending. Looking back, I didn't become an extremely miserly and boring person who was always obsessed with my money. The reality is I spend less time being focused on my money, because I don't worry about it—our finances are under control. Sticking to a budget brings freedom, not slavery.

Before you start building your budget, consider some common advice that applies to six areas of any home's budget.

A Roof over Your Head

The cost of one's home easily gets out of hand. One rule of thumb is never to allow housing costs to exceed 40 percent of your income after taxes. That amount is really too high for most of us in America

Real World Application:

Sticking to a budget brings freedom, not slavery.

to live without financial pressure, though it may be necessary in high-priced areas like Boston, New York, Washington, D.C., or parts of California.

If you own your home, annual repairs and maintenance should equal roughly 1 percent of the value of the house. For instance, if your house is worth $90,000, annual spending of $900 would be normal. Typically, older homes require more, newer homes less. People with time and ability can save a lot of money by making their own repairs. The challenge is making sure you set money aside regularly for maintenance, because expenditures can be infrequent but high.

The Food You Eat

Repairs often can be put off for houses and cars. Clothing can be worn to the point of becoming threadbare. But we need to eat. Some people have a great temptation when it comes to eating out instead of eating at home. If this is a problem in your life, I want to assure you this is not a suggestion that you become a vegetarian and never enter a restaurant or pull into a drive-through. The good news we recommend: No matter how tight you are financially, budget something for recreation and eating out, since you probably will do it anyway. Budget an amount that is reasonable—based on your income—and then make sure you don't overspend.

What a relief! When the Dean family first tried to get a handle on its finances, we cut out everything related to having fun (and that usually includes eating out in middle-income America). The bottom line was—it didn't work.

I'll never forget how grateful I was to hear a financial expert say it was unrealistic to expect to spend nothing on recreation, entertainment, and eating out. In our culture it's almost an impossible goal. The key is to put something in your budget you can afford, and then spend just that amount and no more. That's what Elizabeth and I did, and we don't feel guilty about the money we spend, as long as it's in the budget.

Food for families will cost $100 to $125 per person per month. There are always exceptions, as someone with hungry teenagers will attest. In some parts of the country, like Alaska, expect to pay a lot more. Some people, through couponing and smart shopping, can do better.

> No matter how tight you are financially, budget a reasonable amount for recreation and eating out, then make sure you don't overspend.

Eat well but don't eat lavishly. Figure out ways to make your eating-out part of the budget stretch as much as food from the grocery store. Clip coupons. Some fast-food eateries have special offers on certain nights. Coupon books sold around the country offer two-for-one dinner deals. This is a nice way for couples having "date" nights to try out new places.

The Clothes on Your Back

Most of us don't plan for buying clothes. Americans are impulse buyers, but even at sale prices, we spend more than we realize. The arrival of children in a marriage normally forces us at least to create impromptu budgets before school starts and, in most of the country, for spring and fall. Unless you've gained or happily lost twenty pounds in a short time, we recommend thirty to forty dollars per family member per month.

You may find ways to spend even less. We were fortunate in our family to have grandparents willing to buy the kids' clothes. Birthday and Christmas gift money was used to help buy our own clothes. When you must buy new, buy on sale. Beware of department stores luring you into their credit card system by offering extra discounts if you instantly apply for a store card. If you have trouble with credit, this is certainly a bad move. Department stores aren't all bad. They've been forced the past few years to offer deeper sales to stay competitive with discounters. Some friends of ours do well with the outlet malls springing up around the country. My experience is that the discount usually isn't better than sales closer to home.

If you have the nerve and a little time, try thrift and consignment stores. We have one friend who goes to a jumbo thrift store on her way home from work once a week. She has trained herself to "speed read" past the racks for items she knows her family needs. It's quite a feat, finding the amount of new and almost new clothing she's been able to buy. Nothing is more satisfying than discovering a Neiman Marcus four-hundred-dollar silk dress "on sale" for five dollars. The dress obviously had never been worn, judging from the extra buttons still attached by the manufacturer. That doesn't happen every day, but bargains are available if you have the time to look.

The Cars You Drive

Men seem to be the most likely to have the new car itch. Budgeting for cars is tricky because nothing seems to break down for a while, and then, everything major goes wrong all at once.

The average later-model car should average fifty dollars a month with routine maintenance and repairs. Once a car is past warranty, I recommend seventy-five dollars a month be budgeted for the routine and the unexpected. Remember, I used to be one of those guys interested in image, and that meant borrowing to buy new cars. Now I have a paid-for car with 161,000 miles on it, which is definitely beyond the warranty, and so I put seventy-five dollars per month in the budget for repairs. I'm still better off paying the repairs and saving for another used car than going back into the world of buying cars on credit.

It is common to underestimate expenses in all of the four areas above. The answer is to build your budget and track what you spend for a few months. Then revise the budget to make it more realistic.

Having Yourself a Merry Christmas

I wish we could celebrate Christmas without expensive gift giving. (My wife says I'm just a scrooge.) In our home, we try to put Christ into Christmas, but that doesn't mean we don't enjoy giving gifts, especially to children.

There's just one way of doing this without turning back to those credit cards, which by now you may have cut up and thrown away: Save every month. My high-finance brain always scoffed at those Christmas clubs offered by banks, credit unions, and savings and loans. Not anymore. Don't worry about the low interest. If you can't save for Christmas in your budget, go the club route. Decide how much you want to spend, divide by the number of months until Christmas, and your holiday giving will be provided for. (More on this in chapter 7.)

Taking Your Trip

Many of us like to take at least one big annual vacation. Normally it works this way: Just about the time you finish paying for a financed Christmas, it's time to "heavy up" on the cards again for the summer vacation you feel you so richly deserve.

I'm not suggesting you need an annual getaway to Hawaii or the Bahamas, but I do believe you should try for a time away to relax and recharge. The only way to get out of the credit-card trap is as suggested above—save a little each month. You may not even realize the amount of money a vacation costs. It's not just using a card for hotels and recreation. You may put fuel and other expenses on a gasoline credit card. Put an honest cost on next year's vacation, divide by the number of months until you plan to leave, and then save the necessary amount each month.

Again, there are ways to cut corners, and I'm not just suggesting taking advantage of free nights from a company trying to sell you a timeshare. If you like the outdoors, camping is a great way to vacation. We know of one middle-income family that spent the winter planning next year's vacation. The children were taught geography and helped with research on places to visit. Each year, they covered several states so by the time the children were grown, the family had visited forty-eight states in a pop-up camper the father and children had built. To this day, the grown children can name all the state capitals and recall national parks and forests.

Our family likes to settle in, and that means going back to the same location on the seashore or in the mountains each year. Other members of the extended family join us, and it's a great time to catch up.

Be original. Be creative, and you and your children will have memories to recall the rest of your lives. Good times can be passed on from your children to the next generation.

The Robinsons Create a Budget

One week after my first meeting with the Robinsons, I was a bit surprised to see Mark and Paula show up for our second session. With Mark's impulsiveness and Paula's avoidance of problems, I had suspected they might be no-shows. Mind you, they didn't step briskly up the steps, but they arrived on time, worksheets in hand.

The Robinsons admitted it was still hard to take Step 2 and set up a monthly budget. (I used the word budget reluctantly, since it sends shock waves of personal trauma through many people.) Mark, being the more talkative, was the first to speak. "We had a hard time just sitting down. In fact, even I avoided the task altogether for two days before I finally mentioned it." Paula admitted it had been on her mind, but she didn't want to be the one to bring it up. "I think we were both afraid just to start," she told me.

Once they began, they remembered what I had suggested one week earlier: Don't spend too much time trying to get accurate numbers. Estimate those numbers you don't know for certain. Fine-tune them later.

What Mark and Paula feared would take all night took less than two hours. Listing income was easy. We all seem to know exactly what

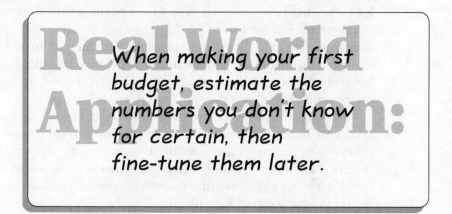

Real World Application: When making your first budget, estimate the numbers you don't know for certain, then fine-tune them later.

we make. Writing down expenses was a little trickier. Thirteen expense categories may seem like a bit much, but by estimating amounts, you can speed up the task considerably. Get through the budget once with a pencil, and you can always fine-tune later.

Here are a few more hints I gave the Robinsons that will also work for you:

- I can't say it too many times: Keep it simple. Don't spend more than two hours or you may never finish. Set a timer for an hour, and if you're not half done, realize you are being too exact.
- Only use net wages instead of gross income. It's the take-home pay that you have to spend, so use that number. If you get paid twice a month or every two weeks, multiply to compute your annual take-home pay and then divide by twelve months. That's the amount you enter under income.
- Other sources of income, even if paid quarterly or annually, should be divided into an estimated monthly amount. Be conservative in your estimate. It's always better to be pleasantly surprised than disappointed with sporadic income.
- If you come out ahead after completing your budget, put money into savings. One of the goals we recommend is to start putting money into savings or significantly increase the amount already being socked away.
- Car insurance and trips to the doctor or dentist don't come up every month. Estimate an annual amount and divide by twelve. If you already are a record keeper, you may want to quickly look up what you spent last year. Don't belabor this. Rough numbers are fine for a start.
- If after putting in all income and expenses you find you are not making enough for what you spend, don't be discouraged. The point of building a budget is to discover where you stand. Some people don't learn until they are forced into bankruptcy.
- On the Robinsons' budget (and the blank budget you will complete), there is a line called Debt Repayment. We encourage everyone to put items here like the Robinsons' car payment. It's put there instead of under Transportation to make it obvious this is an area of choice, not necessity. Later we'll talk about saving and paying cash for cars.

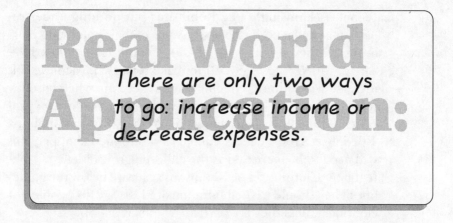

There are only two ways to go: increase income or decrease expenses.

The Robinsons' Unbalanced Budget

The Robinsons came into my office with a budget that showed their spending exceeded their income. This isn't unusual. If you're having trouble with debt, it's probably because you're living beyond your means. Now is the time to get things under control.

The Robinsons were ready to get out the red pencil and make the needed cuts, but they wanted guidance. I explained there are only two ways to go: increase income or decrease expenses.

Decreasing expenses meant making sacrifices in discretionary spending, since other areas were pretty well fixed. Look over the Robinsons' first stab at a budget in figure 3 in appendix A, then read the following notes.

Category 1 (Income): Mark is paid once a month; Paula is paid every two weeks. To get the correct amount for Paula's monthly net wages, take her biweekly paycheck of $274.62 and multiply times 26 to obtain her annual net wages of $7,140.12 (remember she works part time). Her average monthly net wages are found by dividing her annual net wages by 12, or $595.01.

Category 3 (Savings): Mark is having $100 a month withheld from his paycheck for retirement, but his net pay reflects the deduction, so it is not added in this category.

Category 4 (Housing): The Robinsons put nothing under repairs/maintenance. Based on the value of their home ($105,000 in fig. 1), they should have $87.50 a month ($105,000 x 1% = $1050; $1050 ÷ 12 = $87.50) to make repairs. To achieve this increase will require reducing the budget somewhere else.

Category 5 (Food): The Robinsons listed $375 per month for groceries, which puts them under the average ($100 minimum x 4 people = $400). Unless Paula is a disciplined shopper, this will need to be increased as the children grow older.

Category 6 (Clothing): The Robinsons again are below the guideline. They should have a minimum of $120 ($30 x 4 people) for clothing, unless they are particularly smart shoppers.

Category 7 (Transportation): Our model family has two cars, and one is within warranty. They should be budgeting $125 monthly for car repairs ($50 + $75), which puts them below our guideline.

Category 8 (Medical): Mark pays $120 monthly toward his employer-provided health insurance, and this is withheld from his paycheck. We don't list his contribution in the budget because the amount shown for his net wages reflects the deduction.

Category 9 (Children): Private education is a big expense, and it makes everything much tighter. The key is always "What are our priorities?"

Category 10 (Debt Repayment): This number comes from the List of Debts (fig. 2).

Category 11 (Insurance): The Robinsons pay their life insurance once a year. It costs a little less this way, but for most middle-income families it's too hard to come up with this much cash. In this case, a monthly payment plan is best.

Category 12 (Recreation): This includes adult allowances for each of you to spend as you please and entertainment money for the whole family for things like eating out and going to the movies. Adult allowances are much like allowances for the children. They provide pocket money for incidentals and are not accountable to the spouse. They can be used for lunch and small personal needs, or saved for bigger purchases. Both spouses should get the same amount to avoid arguments.

Category 13 (Gifts): Although Christmas comes once a year, the cost should be spread over twelve months.

Category 14 (Other Personal/Business): If the previous categories are properly set up, very little goes here.

Net Margin/Deficit: This number is negative on the Robinsons' first budget. Their goal is to bring it to zero. Any surplus would be added to Giving, Saving, or Debt Repayment.

The Robinsons' Budget Balanced

The next week, Mark and Paula came in with big smiles. They had worked hard to make their budget balance and had wrangled with some hard decisions. Figure 4 in appendix A shows their revised balanced budget.

Category 1 (Income): Mark decided to teach three college courses a year at a university. This would bring in about $5,300 more a year or $4,100 after taxes—a monthly income increase of $340. Mark and Paula decided to halt their monthly retirement plan contributions until their credit cards were paid off. This increased their take-home pay by $100 per month.

Category 2 (Giving): This increased by $40 a month to reflect Mark's income from teaching.

Category 3 (Savings): This decreased by $50 a month after monthly contributions to Paula's IRA halted.

Category 4 (Housing): The Robinsons decided to discontinue cable TV temporarily, saving $20 a month. Resolving to write more, they decreased their long distance phone budget by $20 per month. They added $80 to their home repair and maintenance budget and suspended all home improvements expenditures, saving $50 per month.

Category 6 (Clothing/Grooming): Mark and his son, Carl, decided to get their haircuts at home, saving $20 monthly.

Category 7 (Transportation): Auto repair and maintenance was increased by $50 a month to follow guidelines.

Category 9 (Children): The Robinsons reduced babysitting to zero by joining a babysitting co-op through their church, saving about $15 per month.

Category 10 (Debt Repayment): They increased payments on debts by $70 per month to achieve payoff six months sooner.

Category 12 (Recreation): By taking lunches to work, they trimmed personal allowances by $40. They reduced vacation spending by $70 per month, which will mean fewer trips. Magazine and newspaper subscriptions were reduced by $8 and entertainment by $50 a month with plans for less eating out.

Category 13 (Gifts): Mark and Paula cut $30 a month by resolving to make more gifts. Birthday spending also was reduced.

Net Margin/Deficit: This has been sliced to zero and the goal is achieved!

As you can see, the Robinsons had to make sacrifices and increase their workload. But I could tell by the Robinsons' big smiles that it was all more than worth it to gain some control over their finances.

Now it's time for you to take the plunge. Turn to figure 13 in appendix A. Set aside two hours, find a quiet place, ask for God's help, get a grip on your pencil, and begin! Remember, becoming a good steward of what God has given you is a holy calling. "Commit to the LORD whatever you do, and your plans will succeed" (Prov. 16:3).

WHEN A MOTHER WANTS TO STAY AT HOME

Multitudes of working mothers want to interrupt careers and raise their children full time. Mothers with preschool children especially want to stay home with them.

It may seem impossible at first, but do you know what it would take? To determine if it would be feasible, begin by preparing a budget without the second income. Be realistic. What is the monthly income shortfall? Now reevaluate spending in all areas of the budget. Ask yourself the following questions:

1. Can I generate extra income without having to work outside the home?
2. What expenses could be eliminated if I didn't have to go to work, especially if I could spend time being a wiser shopper and the family were willing to eat out less?

3. What little-used assets could be sold to raise cash for reducing debts and payments?
4. Could the family get by with one car?
5. Could we sell our home and move to one with a smaller mortgage payment?

Does it still seem impossible? Turn it over to God and ask for his wisdom and provision. Establish a game plan for staying home in the future if it isn't possible now.

Elizabeth worked outside the home for many years. We analyzed our budget many times and saw no way we could afford for her to quit. But we set a goal and began working toward it. We missed the goal many times, but we felt strongly that this was what God wanted. We persisted and God provided through a totally unexpected source. As of this writing, Elizabeth has been home for six years. We have had to do without some things and money gets tight at times, but it is worth it.

5

> **ACTION STEP 3:** *Break Out of Plastic Prison Forever*

One Paycheck from Broke

LIVING FROM PAYDAY to payday is no fun. Perhaps you or someone you love has a problem with debt. Perhaps baby boom squeeze is catching up with you. Your income may be high but you've never learned to control spending. The prospect of helping aging parents, sending children to college, and sliding into retirement leaves your stomach in a knot.

In 1985, 30 percent of Americans failed to pay off their credit-card debts each month. In 1995, the figure had risen to 50 percent. This is not a case of finding comfort in numbers. Charge-card fever keeps going up. In 1996, *Money Magazine* reported that installment debt in America, including auto loans and credit card balances, showed a $\frac{1}{3}$ percent increase in the past two years.

Many people finally are beginning to see this as a problem. The expanding personal finance sections of bookstores reflect this growing concern. A few years back you saw titles such as *You Can Have It All* and *Nothing Down*. Today you see more sensible titles like *Your Money or Your Life* and *How to Take Control of Your Finances*.

The secular book market is flooded with "control" books, some of which include personal finance. A new subset follows the theme "you are who you are because of your personality makeup." A popular theory also holds that just as some people are predisposed to alcoholism or gambling, others are predisposed to becoming debtors.

Yet, no matter what the approach, every book that addresses the debt crisis eventually provides action steps that, if followed, will result in a debt-free life. If there were statistics, I think they would show that few people are able to take the steps and walk straight out of debt.

We live in a money-driven world that continues to fine-tune invitations to spend more and worry less. Answering that invitation has led many into a trap they believe they can't escape. The average Christian who arrives at the door of a Cornerstone counselor is buried under sixteen thousand dollars of consumer debt.

LIVING A LIFE OF INTEGRITY AND FREEDOM

Deep down, Christians know that impatient attitudes toward spending are sinful. They try to say no, but the pull of "mammon" seems irresistible. Is there an easy answer? Can I provide you with a simple list of a dozen easy steps to become debt-free? My answer is a resounding no. And if any financial counselor—Christian or non-Christian—ever promises you an immediate cure for debt through three easy steps, the regular purchase of lottery tickets, or even undergoing hypnosis, run away fast.

The way to start is to understand your goal. The overall goal of financial independence is good, but it isn't independence as the world sees it. At Cornerstone, we don't try to lead people to the point where they can spend their lives sipping cocktails on the beach of some dis-

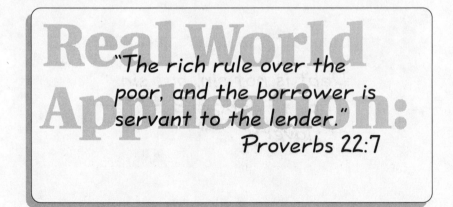

Real World Application:

"The rich rule over the poor, and the borrower is servant to the lender."
Proverbs 22:7

tant island. Our aim is to lead Christians to serve the Lord Jesus Christ with integrity and freedom.

Does the Bible say debt is a sin? Should Christians never borrow money? With the problems debt brings, it's easy to give a simple yes to that question. But the Bible never says borrowing is a sin any more than it says money is evil. But borrowing can be a pitfall.

At any given time in our life we each have a certain amount of money to spend. God has made us stewards over that money, so we have to spend it with integrity. If we habitually live on credit, the cost for us to live will be much higher. It is costlier to obtain something using debt than by saving and paying cash for it. In other words, debt is wasteful.

Integrity enters into debt in a second way, too. When we take on a debt, we make a commitment to pay it back within a certain time. But we don't know for sure that we will be able to meet that commitment. The Book of James warns against the presumption that everything is going to go just the way we plan it (James 4:13–16). We may experience illness, a layoff, or any number of unforeseen events and not be able to honor our commitment.

Behind most large debts is a lifestyle of self-indulgence. The inability to wait for what we want and the attitude that we shouldn't have to wait usually lead to a life of credit. We get into the habit of thinking of desires as needs. Taking the bus to work, living on hamburger instead of steaks, getting shoes resoled instead of buying new ones—these alternatives rarely occur to us. We become masters of rationalization.

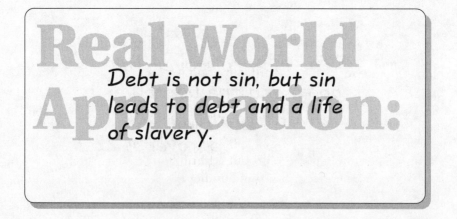

Real World Application:

Debt is not sin, but sin leads to debt and a life of slavery.

Letting desires control us is a form of slavery. Our wants become idols we are trapped into serving. Soon we feel we're beginning to sink under what we owe, but we can't seem to stop spending. It's a miserable way to live. The debt gets so heavy it feels like a constant weight on our shoulders, one we can't seem to reduce. It just keeps on getting heavier.

Some of you may be saying, "That isn't my problem. We aren't self-indulgent. We only spend on necessities, but we still can't even pay for car repairs without using the credit card." If this is your situation, work on implementing the ideas in this book, and with prayer and time, your situation will improve. You must persevere. The changes won't come overnight.

Elizabeth and I made our way out of debt slowly and the process was painful at times. But from the moment we stopped living on credit and began making sacrificial decisions to pay back our obligations, we experienced the peace that comes from a life of integrity and the freedom that comes from smashing our materialistic idols.

Our credit cards were revoked one by one when we found we couldn't make even minimum payments. I had to endure humbling phone conversations with many credit-card representatives. The habit of spending beyond our means underwent a progressive death in us, but that death led to a freedom I love to help others experience. We simply need to know it is possible. The Lord has the power to bring about change in our lives. He's in the business of setting people free.

DEVELOP A PLAN

The key to opening the door to financial freedom is to have a plan. Otherwise, in spite of all your good intentions, you will only be pounding on the door in frustration. I don't know your situation, so I can't help you decide on the details of a debt-reduction plan, but I can offer you two approaches—one of which should work for you.

Approach number one is to put additional money toward debt reduction each month. Approach number two is to sell an asset and reduce the debt.

Let's use Mark and Paula as an example and look at the pros and cons of both approaches. The Robinsons have $16,425 in consumer debt from credit cards and educational loans. By consumer debt I mean all debt incurred over time except for a home mortgage. If you've taken out a home equity loan and used the proceeds for something other than improving your home, I include that loan in the definition of consumer debt. Mark and Paula's monthly payments are $482. You can see this in figure 2.

They could choose the first approach and add $50 or $100 to their monthly payments, or they could take the second approach and sell an asset. In figure 1 you can see their assets. The Robinsons' camper is estimated to be worth $4,500, and Paula's IRA is worth $4,800. Liquidating the IRA would result in a fairly significant loss since it would become taxable income and trigger an additional 10 percent penalty. That leaves the camper—something they regularly enjoy using. So what approach should the Robinsons use to get out of debt, and what should they take into consideration in making their decision?

The question isn't just an economic one. It has three aspects:

Economic: What is the lowest cost for the best return?

Emotional: Can we live with this choice? How will it affect us emotionally?

Spiritual: What is God's view? After study of the Word, prayer, and a deep commitment to obedience, how do we believe the Lord is leading?

Real World Application:

Every economic decision has emotional and spiritual aspects. Ignoring this fact can be a mistake.

For the Robinsons, selling the camper might not be the best decision emotionally. After praying, and realistically facing the difficulty of living without that restful outlet for their stressful lives, the Robinsons decided to make an extra monthly payment of $70 and get out of debt slowly.

Bob and Debbie Schultz have a different set of circumstances. Their debts are listed below. They also decided to pay off their debts by increasing their monthly payments by $100 to $530. Their question is, What do we pay off first? Financially, it would make sense to pay off debt C because it carries the highest rate of interest.

Creditor	Monthly Payment	Remaining Payments	Balance Due	Interest Rate
A. Visa	$170	years	$3,400	18%
B. Discover	$60	years	$500	16%
C. Friendly Finance	$125	22 months	$1,800	22%
D. Parents	$75	4 months	$300	8%
TOTALS	$430		$6,000	

However, if the Schultzes put all their additional payment—one hundred dollars per month—toward their smallest debt first (debt D), it will be paid off in two months. Emotionally this will give their plan great momentum. They can scratch a creditor off their list in just two months! Then they can tackle their next smallest debt (debt B). By putting the entire $175 freed from eliminating debt D toward

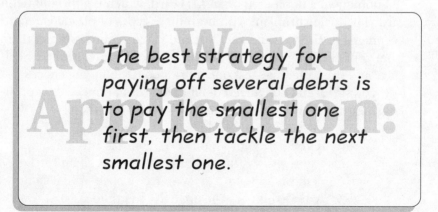

The best strategy for paying off several debts is to pay the smallest one first, then tackle the next smallest one.

that debt along with the $60 they are paying already, they'll be paying $235 per month. When debt B is gone, they will have $235 to add to the $125 they're paying on debt C. Debt A can be paid off last, but by then they will have only one creditor and one debt. Along the way they have seen real progress as one debt after another has been reduced to nothing!

There are several other questions you need to ask: Should you stop using credit cards? Are debit cards okay to use? What should you do if you can't make the minimum payments? What about a consolidation loan? Are credit counseling services any good? What about bankruptcy? What about saving? Let's take them one at a time.

Should I cut the cards?

Elizabeth and I had our credit cards revoked. Many credit counselors advise destroying them so you won't be tempted. My advice is, don't use them until the debt is paid off. It's almost impossible to implement your debt reduction plan if you keep adding to the balance. I have never seen anyone able to do it. You can start using the first credit card you pay off completely if you pay off the balance every month. The first month you can't pay it off—cut the card!

What about debit cards?

Debit cards work just like a credit card on the retail side of the purchase, but instead of creating a debt that you pay later, the amount you charge is subtracted immediately from your checking account. Supposedly their value is that you don't have to carry cash or write a check.

I don't own a debit card or an ATM card, which is a form of debit card. The major problem with both these types of plastic is record keeping. The little receipts get lost and you forget to subtract them from your checking account balance. You don't know your true balance, and from there it's just one more step to bouncing checks.

If you still aren't convinced debit cards are an unnecessary problem, here are a few things you need to know about them:

Liability: If you lose your credit card, your liability for unauthorized purchases is fifty dollars. But, with a debit card, if you don't notify the company within two business days after the loss, your liability can go up to five hundred dollars. Your

> loss could be unlimited if you don't notify the company
> within sixty days of your monthly statement.
> Dissatisfaction: Are you unhappy with your purchase? With a
> credit card you can withhold payment, but with a debit card
> the merchant already has your money.
> Fees: Watch out for annual fees and per-use fees, which can
> range from twenty-five cents to two dollars for each use.

My advice is, if you owe on your credit cards, pay them off and
then use them in the same way you would use a debit card. The first
time you can't pay the balance to zero, get rid of them and pay with
cash or checks.

I realize computers are making electronic transactions more common. But it won't become routine until everyone has a home computer and is comfortable with downloading transactions into the
home computer.

What if I can't make the minimum payments?

This can happen to any of us, once we've allowed ourselves to get
into debt. It may be a temporary financial difficulty or a long-term
problem. When Elizabeth and I were in this situation, we received a
barrage of frightening threats from our creditors to turn us over to
collection agencies. So I picked up the phone, put defensiveness
behind me, and prepared to be honest.

I was able to negotiate a payment less than the minimum amount
due, but things have changed over the last twelve years. Most people
these days can't do what I was able to do. According to Pat Arena,
who is with Consumer Credit Counseling Service in South Florida
and has worked with debtors and creditors for years, minimum payments now are so low most credit-card companies won't go lower.
And if the minimum payments are not made, the company will add
late fees and over-limit fees.

Pat Arena says the best thing to do is write a letter to the company's customer service department telling (1) the history of your
situation, (2) the payment you can make, and (3) why you think the
reduced amount is all you can do. Ask for relief on the late and over-
limit charges. Then faithfully pay the reduced amount on time. If you
get calls from collectors, tell them to look up your account in their

computers. Be polite, but stick to your guns. Collectors have quotas and collecting your debt keeps them on the job.

Should I take out a consolidation loan?

This popular solution has economic and emotional benefits. Unless you go to a "quick loan" service, you can usually negotiate a much lower interest rate. Even if you keep the same monthly payment, the debt will be paid off sooner because more of the payment applies to the principal. Emotionally, it has the advantage of reducing the number of creditors from many to one.

A real trap I have seen countless people fall into with consolidation loans is "yo-yo" borrowing. Break your debt habit first or you will begin building up a credit-card balance again that you can't pay off each month. I recommend you live six months without any new charges before taking out a consolidation loan. Otherwise, you will end up with a consolidation loan payment and credit-card payments, too.

Are credit counseling services worth their salt?

If you think it would help emotionally to have an intermediary between you and your creditors, and you can make at least some payments each month, a non-profit credit counseling service might help. They will communicate with creditors for you and handle your payments. They will stop the annoying phone calls from collectors and they can get concessions from creditors on fees you may not be able to negotiate. Beware of debt-reduction services or bankruptcy lawyers advertising on television. Legitimate services usually charge little or no fees because the creditors support them.

Is bankruptcy an option for a Christian?

I'm going to be controversial. I think bankruptcy may be necessary in extreme circumstances. Sometimes creditors can force someone into bankruptcy, and sometimes the emotional pressure can have a severe impact on health. This option should not be pursued without serious prayer and consideration.

However! Just because the debt has been forgiven legally doesn't mean we are relieved of the responsibility of paying it back. Once God has restored our finances, we should make a plan to pay back these debts as we would any other debt. When we took on the debt, we made a covenant to pay it back, and the creditor loaned us money based on our good-faith commitment. As Christians called to wit-

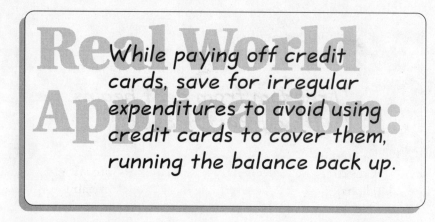

While paying off credit cards, save for irregular expenditures to avoid using credit cards to cover them, running the balance back up.

ness to an unsaved world, we should not consider that covenant nullified by bankruptcy.

Should I save while paying off my debt?

Your debt-reduction plan will never work unless you're saving at the same time. The only way to break the debt cycle is to have money set aside for irregular expenditures that can wreck your budget and drive you back to using credit cards. In a later chapter I'll talk about how to develop a savings plan to go along with your debt-reduction plan. It's the only way to get out of debt and stay out of debt.

CHRISTIANS DON'T GET OUT OF DEBT ALONE

As Christian thinker James M. Boice puts it, "Christians today have secular minds in a secular world." How can we break free? How can we begin to live differently?

A small segment of people may have the sheer determination and personality traits to end indebtedness. I've met some who have done it out of raw fear. But there is no reason to attempt to change borrowing habits on your own.

Freedom from debt begins with earnest prayer. Christians have overworked the word and underutilized the power of prayer. We so easily slip into "I'll be praying for you" and "You can count on my prayers" when we so little understand the concept, much less the power God makes available to his children. He pleads with us to pray.

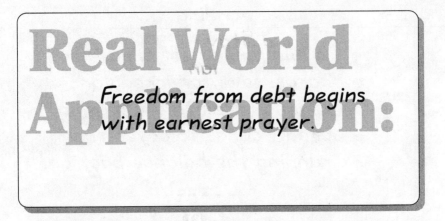

He commands us to pray. And he promises over and over again to answer our prayers. Develop your debt-reduction plan in prayer. Ask for God's help to see you all the way to the end. And as you undergo deliverance from a debt-lifestyle, remember to call out to God whenever you are discouraged or tempted.

God also uses other Christians to help you make it to freedom. My associate, and the founder of Cornerstone, Jim Underwood, spent a decade conducting a highly successful financial seminar for Christians across the country. He noticed that the same people often came back a second time. He discovered that just attending his seminar and reading self-help books didn't solve their problems. After much prayer, Jim closed the seminar business and began counseling people one-to-one from his Orlando office. He offered them three years of accountability at an affordable price. In that time, with God's help, even the hardest cases of professional seminar attenders and book readers were able to change.

6

Going Bust
in a Credit Boom

MOST TOURISTS with the time
will make the trip to a remarkable rock formation outside Atlanta
called Stone Mountain, especially if they have children. The light-
gray granite edifice is larger than, although quite similar to, Mount
Rushmore in South Dakota. This largest stone mountain in North
America appears flat on top. When I was a child, you could walk on
the top, and what had appeared to be flat from below would begin
to slope dangerously downward. Over the years, unsuspecting visitors would walk too far and suddenly find themselves stuck because
the return was too steep. Several people died from falling over the
edge. To prevent tourists from reaching that point of no return, the
park service installed a fence and posted danger signs.

People need warnings, don't they? Just as visitors to Stone Mountain need a fence for their protection, we need financial boundaries
for our protection. Unless we monitor what we spend, we won't be
able to stay on budget and find freedom from debt. It is so easy to
spend money in discretionary areas, and then a week later have to
use our credit card to pay for something essential. We especially need
protection from the constant invitations we receive to spend beyond
our income. Monitoring our spending and comparing it with our

budget also gives us the ability to save every month to meet our long-term financial goals.

I realize people buy a book like this hoping for easy solutions. I also know people don't always read an entire chapter. I hope you will push all the way through this chapter, even if you want a quick fix. If you do nothing else suggested in this chapter, keep reading and try out the first approach.

THE SIMPLEST STARTING POINT EVER INVENTED

This tracking method is so simple it's ridiculous. You may have heard of it. As I share this with clients or in seminars, everybody seems to have had an Aunt Millie or an Uncle Roy who used it all through life.

As Elizabeth and I were going through our "if we just had a little more money, everything would be all right" stage, I met with the president of our bank. This wasn't just anybody. He and my father were members of the Rotary Club. Mr. Deveroux had known me since I was a teenager. The conversation went something like this:

Jim: (palms sweating) Good morning, Mr. Deveroux, how are you today?
Banker: Jim, thanks for asking, I'm quite well. What may I do for you?
Jim: Well, Elizabeth and I seem to be experiencing some short-term financial difficulties, and I need a loan for one thousand dollars to tide us over.

Keep in mind, this was a southern small-town bank. I expected no difficulties in getting money from this longtime family friend. A no-collateral signature loan should have been forthcoming. Was I surprised!

Banker: Jim, I am not going to lend you the money. It would be a disservice. Have you ever heard of the envelope system?

| Jim: | (quite embarrassed, red-faced, swallowing hard, but still acting polite) Why no, I haven't. |

Mr. Deveroux explained how the envelope system works. It took several weeks before my CPA pride allowed me to admit this simple system might be worth a try. We put the envelope system into place and to this day use it faithfully.

So how does the envelope system work?

1. Buy the cheapest envelopes you can find. Better yet, look for old, yellowed envelopes around the house.
2. Pocket money is a big black hole. Give yourself and all family members a monthly allowance.
3. Prepare an envelope for each spending area from your budget that can be conveniently paid in cash, including your allowances.
4. Put the budgeted amount of cash into each envelope. Do this once or twice a month. The system should become routine. Grocery money goes into the food envelope, entertainment money goes into the entertainment envelope, and so on.

Use the envelope system for each budget category in which you can conveniently use cash. It's good to involve the whole family in this process. The simple use of envelopes to control your cash needs will become a major step in tracking and controlling spending.

When the money is gone, the spending stops. This may sound cruel, but it works and is a great way to teach children and parents how not to squander money. The method puts an absolute ceiling on spending, and it simplifies record keeping.

For example, suppose a family sets up a cash envelope for entertainment and eating out. Once a month, seventy dollars goes into the envelope. When the family goes out to eat, the cash to pay for the meal comes from the envelope with the seventy dollars. When the seventy dollars is gone, the spending stops until next month. If the family expects to spend more than seventy dollars in a month because of something special, money from the previous month is held over for the special occasion.

From my experience, this approach draws a family into a game-like effort to make an envelope last longer, especially when the money runs out early the first month or two. Videos are returned on time. Family members start sniffing out coupon deals for eating out. Expensive meals become rare. Impulse buying subsides. The system works as long as everyone in a family is committed to making it work. My message is: Don't cheat!

Envelopes have numerous uses. My family uses envelopes for groceries, gasoline, haircuts, dry cleaning, and, of course, entertainment and eating out. We find it more convenient to pay for certain things with cash, because there is no check to write and track, and there's no credit-card bill to pay the next month. We draw the cash from our checking account by writing a check. This also can be done with an

> **Real World Application:** ATM cards are dangerous if you have problems keeping a spending record and spending what's not part of your budget. If either is the case, put the card away or give it up.

automatic teller machine withdrawal. As I said in the last chapter, don't use the ATM card if you have difficulty keeping a record. We record in the checkbook register how we plan to use the cash and, for our records, treat the money as being already spent. We make sure the money in the envelope is spent in its intended category. If we must borrow from another envelope when money is short, we make sure to pay it back.

In his book *Master Your Money,* Ron Blue points out that purchasing with cash instead of credit cards usually will reduce spending significantly, because most of us find it more difficult to pay cash at the register than to pull out the credit card. I find this true for me and most of our clients. When I know I only have so much cash to carry me through the month, I am more likely to question whether I need to make the purchase. If I buy then, and later wish I had saved my money for something more important, I regret having spent impulsively. "Cash only" is a powerful way to learn not to overspend, and I don't feel deprived because my spending is capped.

The envelope system has built-in limits that teach us self-control, but credit cards are a different story. When my first American Express card came, I was so proud, so self-important, so assured that I could buy the world. You might discover, as I did, that a credit card easily becomes an idol. Once you implement the envelope system, you will be more than ready to start tracking your spending, including your use of credit cards.

But before we deal with a step-by-step approach, we should talk more about credit cards. They are major contributors to debt in our country today. Conquer the cards and you will almost always conquer debt.

PHILOSOPHICAL DIRT ON CREDIT CARDS

If you are over thirty, you probably remember receiving one of those personalized letters from American Express offering you, one of the chosen few, the "privilege" of becoming the holder of a green card. If you accepted, and passed a credit check, you received vanity-stroking invitations to upgrade to a gold card. If you lived in an affluent zip code and showed up on mailing lists with a high income, the embossing was deeper and foil-stamping more pronounced, inviting you to "accept" the platinum card, a real upgrade for a mere few hundred dollars a year.

That first green card invitation stood the test of time. American Express used it for years to gain new members, and only recently has the response rate begun to fall as competition has increased from Discover, MasterCard, and Visa. The allure of credit has become more complex. The only good thing about the travel and entertainment cards is that they must be paid off each month. Yet they foster the same buy-now pay-later philosophy as any other charge card.

The rationale that started the massive use of credit cards was that you don't have to carry as much cash and they help you keep better records. Most of us think of the cards as assets, but they are really only a convenience. Obtaining a gold card will not bring anyone more respect. Credit cards don't provide money. They simply provide a way to borrow money we will need to pay back later. Credit cards are really debt cards. Reality sets in with this change in vocabulary.

The danger of using cards is that we can be fooled into thinking we have more money. In reality each dollar charged will cost that much more in interest over the next year if not paid in full each month. If your credit-card interest rate is 18 percent, then each $1,000 charged over a year becomes $1,180 to be paid back. The payback becomes higher the longer you wait to pay the bill.

The *Chicago Tribune* (Sunday, October 29, 1995) reported that "after paying for housing, food and taxes, Americans spend nearly 90

Real World Application:

Credit cards are really debt cards.

percent of their remaining income on other debts. That number has never been higher and it leaves little for a rainy day."

Banks and credit-card companies have pushed us further into debt in the past few years. Consumers have obliged by delaying debt payback and piling up more interest. Banks have discovered that competing for more debt customers has backfired. Millions of dollars in bad debts are having to be written off. Credit-crazy consumers don't have the money to pay back their easily acquired debts.

Many Americans accepted telephone and mail offers for new credit cards without reading the fine print. They didn't notice that after six months or a year, the initially low interest rate would be higher than that of their current credit cards. They also didn't see that interest started accumulating the day of the purchase, not twenty-five days later. If you don't know how much interest is charged by what method on your current credit cards, call the toll-free number on the back of your cards and ask for a full explanation. Take notes and compare. If you are still confused by what you are paying for credit, seek other help. Make an appointment with a banker and carry along your credit-card statements. A banker will be happy to explain your interest and billing charges in easy-to-understand language. My recommendation is to never accept credit offers by telephone.

Credit-card companies continue to become more sophisticated. Spending, psychographic, and demographic patterns are finding their way into highly complex computer models that allow companies to send you offers they think you are more likely to accept. All I can say is to beware of accepting any new credit.

The director of the Credit Research Center at Purdue University, Michael Staten, has tracked consumer debt loads for years. He says, "Total consumer debt has been growing at a double-digit annualized rate since 1992. But, only in the past nine to 12 months (1995) has the burden of that debt begun to take a deeper bite."

For the most part, credit-card companies use a method of charging you by a principle of thirty-six. The concept is to keep you always paying so the thirty-six-month period never ends. Here's how it works: call Visa after making the suggested minimum payment. Ask how many months it will take to pay off the bill. The answer will be thirty-six months. Call back the next month after making another payment and ask the same question. Logic tells us the answer should be thirty-five months. Wrong. You will be told you have thirty-six months to pay off the balance.

Most credit-card companies charge you each month one-thirty-sixth of the principal balance. Say you have a balance of $1,500 and your MasterCard interest is 21 percent. By paying the minimum, you will need sixty-three months and an extra $503 of interest before you finally receive the statement that says you owe no more.

I share this to turn up the heat, hoping you will decide this is the time to start tracking your expenses to move your debt load to zero. Acquiring things we don't need when we can't afford them results in much more anxiety than if we become people who say no and do without. I became so sick of the debt cycle that I decided to quit using credit cards. We made the commitment to wait until we had the funds, even for essential items. We stuck to it and depended on God to provide.

As you begin to pay off credit-card debts, consider the following tips:

1. Put your credit cards on ice. Don't use them until the credit balances read zero.
2. If you have a problem in running up purchases faster than they can be paid each month, find the scissors and put a quick end to your problem.
3. If that's too much of a shock, put them in a safety deposit box or lock them away and give the key to a friend or relative. If you've had cards canceled because of nonpayment, please don't rush out and find new credit cards.
4. If you are convinced you must have a credit card for business or travel, go down to a single card for those purposes. Record keeping is much easier. Gas stations take bank charge cards.
5. Some cards are still available without an annual fee, especially as your credit improves.
6. If you have sought out a card charging low interest rates, beware.

How to Track Cards and Expenses

You are entering the heart of this chapter. I wrestled with numerous "systems" and read everything I could find on the topic. My goal was to find a method to track expenses and credit cards that would make me think about my spending without becoming obsessed with the task. The record keeping couldn't take much time but had to be done frequently.

My recommendation is to record actual spending twice a week, which should take only ten to fifteen minutes each time. All of us are busy, and we can all think of a million reasons not to embark on the tracking system. But in the long run, you will have saved yourself from messes that seem to take years off your life, messes like bounced checks, missed investment opportunities, and the inability to help others because you have nothing to share.

Today, if I let the tracking fall behind, I find myself making incorrect conclusions about what I've been spending. My mind plays tricks on me, and as a result, I make financial decisions that are not based on reality. One example of how this has occurred in my life is with car repairs. When I didn't track the money we were spending for repairs, it seemed extremely high. I began to get the find-another-car itch. I was mistakenly convinced maintenance costs were too high and it was time to trade or buy.

Three questions come to mind when we track where our money goes:

1. Is our total spending within our income? If not, tracking allows us to do something about it before it gets out of hand.
2. Are we spending more than we thought we were in particular areas? If so, why, and what should we do about it? Is the

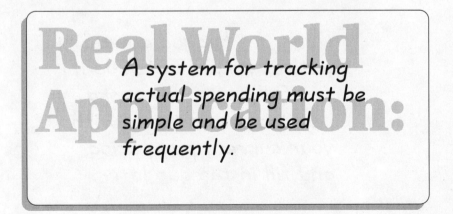

A system for tracking actual spending must be simple and be used frequently.

amount we budgeted unrealistic, or have we lost control of spending?

3. How much of a surplus did we generate for savings or paying extra toward retiring debt?

Some people never start record keeping out of fear they will fall behind. New habits are rarely formed overnight. If you start and fall behind, you may begin to feel guilty and say to yourself, "I really do need to catch up." If this happens, it will take more than ten or fifteen minutes to become current. You will need more time to record the past. This is where people may quit and consider the project a failure. The solution is to forget the past. Start again and don't worry about the gap. After you are back on track and are faithfully recording and comparing expenses to budget, then you might want to take the time to go back and fill in the gap.

Look at the long term. Holes in your record keeping will make it difficult to compare what actually happened with your budget. However, over time you will develop the habit, see the benefits, and feel the impact this will have on your life.

The envelope system described previously is an integral part of my tracking system. As was already pointed out, a tracking system must be simple and used frequently. It also must be easy to implement and maintain. Of all the tracking systems I have investigated, the easiest and simplest one requires using your checkbook register.

> *Don't get bogged down with trying to catch up if you fall behind in record keeping. Start again with your current pay period and fill in the gap later.*

Once in a while, we meet a new client who looks puzzled when we mention the term checkbook register. If that happens, we know without asking that the client probably never balances a monthly bank statement. We explain that the register is the booklet that comes with each new order of checks. This is the place to record checks written and bank deposits made, and to reconcile a bank statement each month.

If you run out of room in your register or you want to start fresh, your bank will happily give you more registers at no charge. If you are one of those people who insists on buying a new jogging outfit before starting a running program, you could go ahead and buy what's called a ledger at any office supply store. They look nice, but you don't really need one to start. Just use what came with your checks and save money even as you begin record keeping.

Once you have the checkbook register and photocopies of the few other forms in appendix A, you are ready.

Step 1: Begin today. Record all deposits and checks in your checkbook register. If you have trouble remembering to record checks, order duplicate (or carbon copy) checks so you always have a copy in your own handwriting. Keep ATM slips and credit card slips in one place on you (your wallet or pocketbook) and in one place at home. Never deviate from those locations. If you still lose the ATM slips, remember what we said earlier and quit using the card.

Step 2: Categorize all deposits and checks in your checkbook register into the fourteen categories of your estimated budget (see figure 5 in appendix A for example).

Step 3: Record deposits and checks for the month onto the two-page Monthly Income and Spending form (fig. 14; see fig. 6 for example). Total each column.

Step 4: On the Comparison of Budgeted to Actual Income and Expenditures form (fig. 15; see fig. 7 for example), record your monthly income and the budgeted monthly amount for each of the thirteen expense categories. Then record your actual month totals for all fourteen categories from the Monthly Income and Spending form.

Step 5: On the Comparison form (fig. 15), find the amount in column C by subtracting column B from column A for all fourteen categories. If your spending is higher than your budget, put the amount in brackets in column C, indicating it is unfavorable.

Step 6: Compute the year-to-date favorable (or unfavorable in brackets) on the Comparison form, indicating spending problems in certain categories.

Did I lose you? If I did, don't quit. Read the steps again, and when I refer to a form, stop and find the form in appendix A. If you are a more visual person, spend a few moments looking at the forms, using the example of the Robinson family. Read the following notes for figures 5–7 to get a feel for how one family uses these forms. If the Robinson and the Dean families can use the forms, you can too! And remember, it keeps getting easier.

Notes for Checkbook Register (fig. 5)

1. After each entry in the checkbook register has been categorized into one of the fourteen groups as in figure 5, record the amount in the appropriate column of the Monthly Income and Spending form.

2. Remember my suggestion to do this twice a week, and it should take no more than fifteen minutes for entering categories in your checkbook register and in the Monthly Income and Spending form (fig. 6).

3. To simplify record keeping, new credit-card purchases are not shown in spending until the bill is paid. If you are making any purchases during the month using a credit card, you will need to record what you are paying for when you make your monthly payment. On the second page of the register in figure 5, you will see a payment to Citibank Visa. The check was written for $236.70, and the amount paid represents a number of items. To record the payment, you will need to take the monthly statement and place each item on the statement into one of the thir-

teen expense categories. The summary in the checkbook register represents the categories affected.

Notes for Monthly Income and Spending Form (fig. 6)

1. Sometimes it's important to see how much has been spent in the categories before the end of the month. In figure 6 a total has been determined about midway through the month, and then the final total is calculated at the end of the month. Look at column 1, Income. The Robinsons brought home $3,075.04 before mid-month, and later the monthly total was $3,349.66.
2. To remain aware of where money is spent, remember to enter all the categorized items from your checkbook register into the Monthly Income and Spending form (fig. 14) twice a week.

Notes for the Comparison Form (fig. 7)

1. Figure 7 compares what has been spent by category to what we planned to spend in our estimated budget. This is important for informing us how close we came to our spending plan. There are columns for the Monthly Favorable (Unfavorable) and the Year-to-Date Favorable (Unfavorable).
2. Monitor trends over several months, since cash flows are not going to fit a nice, consistent pattern and will show some difference from your estimated budget. The key question is, are the unfavorable months offset by the favorable months, or is there a year-to-date trend of a growing unfavorable balance?
3. Look at the year-to-date differences for the Robinsons in figure 7. Based on the size of the differences, spending seems under control for all categories.
4. The entries on the budget to actual in figure 7 are rounded to dollars, showing no cents. This is another way to simplify the procedure by making the math easier.

Well, you made it. But before we go on to the next chapter, let's dig a little deeper with a natural question that arises: Should I reallocate funds when expenses are reduced?

Reallocating Funds

Once your budget is balanced and you are living within your means, more opportunities will come along to reduce spending. They may range from as little as ten dollars a month after changing auto insurance companies to seventy-five dollars a month from clipping coupons and watching for specials at the supermarket.

If it is a legitimate saving, and not the case of shifting what you spend to some other category, plan where you would like to reallocate freed-up funds. Make sure you don't increase spending somewhere else for no good reason. For example, suppose you reduced spending by fifty dollars a month, and you use the savings to add thirty dollars to your children's college fund, increase giving to your church by ten dollars a month, and increase personal allowances for you and your spouse by ten dollars monthly. The enjoyment will only come because you have consciously made these changes.

If you live on a really tight budget, that fifty-dollar savings easily could be absorbed by something else, such as taxes or higher insurance rates. If this happens, thank God that at least you didn't have to cut back in other areas that had little room for discretionary spending. Sometimes it doesn't seem fair, but remember that God is in control, and we need to let him use finances to shape our spiritual walk.

Faithful tracking over time will help you find additional ways to make reallocating funds work.

More Ways to See Results

1. *Both spouses must stay informed.*
    If you are married, you must continue to work hard at discussing what is happening financially. If only one spouse practices cash management and does a marvelous job of keeping track of everything, the system will fall apart if the other has not agreed and does not take part. We recommend couples go over the tracking charts each month together. They can rejoice when the budget is met.
2. *Communication leads to healthy compromise.*
    One side of the marriage can't make all the decisions. God made two people one in marriage, which means they should be

of like mind. Even if a spouse is not prone to communicate, keep communicating anyway. If there isn't communication and compromise, the day will come when a serious argument erupts.

3. *When shopping for nonperishables, wait a couple of days before making the purchase.*

   I enjoy spending money when I have it, a tendency that got me into trouble years ago. Although that desire has lessened, the temptation is still there. When I'm shopping and see just the "right" item, I will wait two or more days before going back. I also pray for God's guidance about the purchase, and if the desire lessens over the two days, I don't buy it. Frequently, I have forgotten about my desire to purchase the item after a couple of days. This is a good exercise for children, who are often more prone than adults to buy impulsively.

4. *If you buy clothing and you are tighter than tight, hang the item in your closet where you can see it easily for a few days before removing the tag.*

   If you still want it after a few days, keep it. Otherwise, take the sales receipt and return the merchandise.

5. *Delay other purchases for a month or more.*

   If you need an item but can wait a couple of months, do so, even if you have the money. That snowblower or computer may be priced lower if you decide to wait. You may later conclude you didn't need it after all, because you have been getting by just fine without it. This has happened to me many times.

6. *If after budgeting and tracking you see there is no way to eliminate the deficit, consider selling an asset.*

   When this happened to us, we made a serious decision. We had two cars, both financed. We sold one car and used that money to replace it with another car for cash. Yes, I traded down, but by doing so, we came closer to meeting our budget.

7. *Establish personal spending allowances, just like your children's allowance, to set up needed boundaries.*

   This has been one of the most helpful things we've ever done.

In our case, we still needed more to make ends meet. We decided to sell our house, expecting it to take at least three or four months because the market was so slow. But God was moving to help us meet our goals. Just two days after we signed the Realtor's contract, our first looker offered us close to our asking price in cash. We took it and found a house to rent for half the amount of our monthly mortgage payment. In a remarkably short time, our financial pressure had been significantly relieved.

Once our Cornerstone clients have budgeted and tracked outgo and income for a few months, they usually wonder how long to keep using this approach. My answer may sound discouraging. How long should you practice tracking? Forever.

That may sound harsh. But give this program six months and ask yourself the question again. I think you will be sold on this newfound freedom.

I employ one other form of managing our finances, because God has not totally delivered me from anxiety. Look at appendix C to learn how to project cash needs for the month. This is helpful for those of us who have variable incomes. If you live off a home-based business or are self-employed, look in the back of the book and decide whether, like me, you will benefit from this additional step.

```
ACTION
STEP 5:  Save Monthly
         for Nonmonthly
             Needs
```

7

Rainy Days and Somedays

MY EYES WERE straining, watching a herd of elk grazing on summer grass above the tree line. I blinked, my eyes shifted down, caught by the quick movements of a chipmunk asking for a handout. He settled his request on a young girl, probably no more than ten, pretty with her well-brushed, long brown hair. Her ruddy cheeks framed a smile of contentment as she drank what I noticed was a store-brand soda taken from an ice chest in the trunk of the family car, a seventies-something green Plymouth.

Now I was intrigued, unable to stop observing the scene as this youngster was joined by members of her family, sharing a vacation at Rocky Mountain National Park in Colorado. Two brothers and a sister came first, then the parents. They had traveled far, the Michigan license plate revealed, to enjoy the rare mountain air and unmatched beauty of thirteen-thousand-feet-high Trailridge Road.

I began making guesses about them. From the age of the car and style of clothing, they had to be middle-income. I pictured all six camped a few thousand feet below, living under the pines in a large tent, cooking most of their meals on a borrowed Coleman stove. They had to be Christians. They were too happy to be anything else. No new car and none of the latest children's designer clothes, but a long memory-packed vacation to an awe-inspiring spot without the luxuries that run up credit-card debts . . . this family obviously had made choices. Here was a family better off for having said no to some things to capture a taste of God's creation.

Such a trip must have started months before. It required cash, and cash for a middle-income family comes by saving. Remember elementary school and the stories of the squirrel? Building the nest, collecting, and storing food were the only ways to survive an approaching winter. Saving may not seem like fun at the time. But the rewards, as this family found, could be exceedingly pleasant and guilt-free.

We need to save for several expenses that don't appear every month. The big six are car repairs, insurance, medical expenses, household repairs, Christmas, and of course, vacations. Budgets are wrecked by any of these holes in one's pocket. As I mentioned, it can take half a year or longer to recover from a financed Christmas and the rest of the year to pay off a "charged" vacation. There is an easy solution: Treat occasional expenses as if they occur every month, and set the money aside for when they arrive.

This is the only way to deal with an air conditioner that costs $650 to repair in the heat of July. Only saving will see you through getting cool and the simultaneous need for a root canal and matching crown costing $800.

> Real World Application:
>
> *Treat occasional expenses as if they occur every month, and set the money aside for when they arrive.*

RAINY DAYS

Setting Up a Cash Reserve

The accounting term for money saved for rainy days is cash reserve. So let's go about setting up this cash reserve to see you through the planned and the unexpected.

First, identify areas in your budget that don't come up every month. Turn to figure 4 in appendix A and look again at the Robinsons' budget. Mark and Paula don't buy clothes (category 6) every month, but notice there is an allocation of seventy dollars. By setting aside money each month in savings to buy clothes, they find it's easy to reimburse their checking account when they do make a purchase. You do the same thing for home repairs/maintenance (category 4), car repairs (category 7), life insurance (category 11), vacations (category 12), and gifts (category 13).

The Robinsons participate in a health maintenance organization (HMO) and have dental insurance, otherwise they would also need to set aside money every month for medical expenses (category 8).

Budgeting a small amount each month for occasional expenses has the effect of smoothing out the cash needs of a family. You may want to set up an extra checking or savings account for the cash reserve. Here's how it works.

Look at the checkbook register of figure 8 in appendix A. A total of $340 is transferred to cash reserve this month, with the amounts broken down: clothing $70 and car repairs $80, for example. We will categorize the transfers as number 3 for savings, since the Robinsons aren't spending the money right now.

Figure 9 shows the cash reserve account with appropriate amounts for each category. Transferring the $340 from regular checking increases the total balance. At the same time, the amount you budget is added to each category.

This same example (fig. 9) helps you see that you need to take money from the cash reserve account and put it back into your checking account as it is used. You never know when you may need to find the balance in a certain category. Notice the new total. Sometimes a category is negative because spending is ahead of what you planned, such as with clothing here. If this is temporary, that's fine. If every month for several months the category goes into the red, you need to increase your budget amount or spend more time planning how to cut back.

Let's look at another example. The checkbook register in figure 5 shows spending in several of the areas for which we have set aside funds in the cash reserve. For example, check 440 on September 12 to J.C. Penney for $48 and check 452 on September 22 to Smith's Amoco for $112.28 should be reimbursed from the Clothing and Car Repairs categories in Cash Reserve (fig. 9). Check 447 on September 17 to Citibank Visa also includes a payment of $92.60 for clothing, which needs to be reimbursed from the cash reserve. Look again at figure 8. It shows a reimbursement to checking from the Clothing category for $141 ($48 + $92.60 rounded). The reimbursement is shown as coming out of category 3, which is removing it from savings.

Here's a final example: In figure 5, there is a check for $58.75 to Wal-Mart (446) that includes $35.56 for home maintenance, a check for $236.70 to Citibank Visa (447) that includes $31.61 for home maintenance, a check for $32.65 to Home Depot (450) also for home maintenance, and a check for $28.41 to Service Merchandise (453) for a gift. Figure 8 shows a reimbursement to checking from Cash Reserve for each of these payments.

As you begin setting aside funds in your cash reserve (fig. 16 is a blank form for you to use), the balance begins to grow. As it grows, you may begin to think you are better off than you are. This is not money to spend as you wish. It is set aside to cover specific future expenses.

> Rainy days will always come. The temptation is powerful after a few months of saving to spend these funds for something different. Spend them and you are back where you were before implementing this action step.

It's Worth the Work

It may seem that this cash reserve system requires a lot of work. But it's worth it.

The Gore family knows from experience. Dave works in the medical field and earns $42,000 a year. When Debby delivered their first of two children, they decided she would quit her job. Overnight, the Gores entered the minority status of single-income families. They were not making ends meet when they heard from a friend about Cornerstone.

We quickly found they were $227 in the red. What to do? Increasing their income was out of the question. We could lower some expenses, but with costs of the two children, cutting back was not a total answer. You see, the Gores had piled up $19,000 in consumer debt. Paying $373 a month would require the next five and a quarter years before the monthly statement would say zero owed.

The next question was, Is there an asset that could be sold? The answer was yes. Dave and Debby owned a piece of property worth $30,000 on which they hoped someday to build their dream home. We didn't make a recommendation at the budget meeting; we challenged them to go home and pray. They did and came back the next week with a firm conviction the Lord wanted them debt-free. The property sold, allowing the Gores to pay off the consumer debt and put $11,000 in savings. Ask them today and they are still convinced this was the right decision. Without the monthly debt payments, the Gores were able to set up a workable budget taking into account nonmonthly expenses, which meant that they didn't need to dip into their $11,000 savings, even with new expenses from having the children.

How Not to Blow a Windfall

Sometimes we receive an unexpected amount of money. It could be a gift, a tax refund, or an inheritance. One financial planner has noticed that people who spend the money for a luxury item they normally can't afford run into even more trouble later. People buy an expensive car or stereo system and raise their standard of living beyond their means. They begin to fund silver spoon tastes with debt.

An easy way to prevent this is to wait. Wait before deciding what to do with the unexpected bonus. If you wait a month, I guarantee you will have a more stable mind on what to do. If the windfall is greater than three thousand dollars, wait even longer, maybe three months. Make this a matter of prayer, and consider putting the money

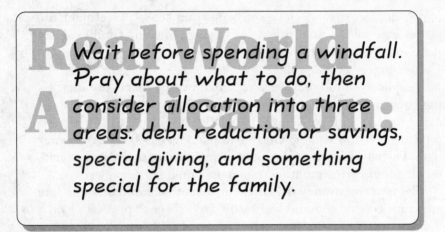

Wait before spending a windfall. Pray about what to do, then consider allocation into three areas: debt reduction or savings, special giving, and something special for the family.

toward debt reduction or savings, special giving, and buying something special for the family.

Look at these areas more closely:

1. *Debt reduction or savings.*
   How can some of this money best be used to accelerate your debt reduction or savings efforts?
2. *Giving beyond normal giving.*
   How might you give above and beyond regular offerings for a special need? Has God placed something special on your hearts? Let the entire family participate. There are few greater joys than passing on your blessing to someone else.
3. *Something special for the family.*
   Is there something you always wanted to do or buy that you never could afford? This might be the right time.

By splitting the money three ways, you balance how the money is used. You feel good about accelerating the accomplishment of important goals. You experience joy from special giving, and you are able to spend some of the money for the family's enjoyment.

Whether you divide the money into thirds doesn't matter so much. Your decision may depend on how much money came unexpectedly. I always favor putting the greatest amount toward debt reduction and savings.

Depleted Cash Reserve

While building a cash reserve, you may not be able to accumulate enough before a car or house repair wipes out what you saved, and you might not even cover all the cost. Or, because you are still paying off last Christmas, you may not be able to save enough for the next yuletide. This is not uncommon, and it tests your commitment to staying out of debt. You can do one of two things: Cut back on Christmas for one year to catch up on your savings, or put part of the spending on a credit card. If you go the route of the credit card, make certain you have a strict budget so you don't overspend, and increase your get-out-of-debt payment schedule if possible. Remember, our goal before God is to treat credit cards as a truly last resort. We want to pay off and stay out of debt.

Once you are in the habit of paying from what you have, you will begin to enjoy and even crave the peace of knowing you won't have to take months to pay for something that will eventually be gone or worn out. Our riches are in Jesus Christ, not in the things of this passing world. God has promised to meet our needs. When we refocus our hearts on him and we remember his blessings, it's much easier to live with less. Life becomes more joyful.

SOMEDAYS

Budgeting for Vacations

Take all the big six items and work with them just as you do in planning for a vacation. Most of us don't know how much a summer vacation will really cost. Without that knowledge another budget-wrecker will strike.

At our house, we involve the entire family. Since I've been tracking vacation expenses for several years, I know fairly closely what a trip will require. You may not remember every expense the first time, but plunge ahead like I did.

When we decide where we want to go, I set up a special budget. Determine an average amount you will spend on lodging, meals, and recreation. Gasoline depends on the number of miles you will be driving. Budget slightly higher than you expect.

As you use the new system, don't be foolish. A family I know has tracked expenses for years and set aside money for the unexpected. Before taking a winter vacation in the Rockies, this family was one month away from having enough money saved to buy a new set of tires, but decided to take the vacation with the old tires. Three flats later, the family found itself in a little-populated area where tire bargains were unknown. So be wise as well as prudent.

At the Dean home, we know how much there is to spend, and let our children make choices about our vacations. Do we eat cereal for breakfast and sandwiches for lunch so we can enjoy nicer meals out in the evening? Do we stay in a motel that provides a free continental breakfast so we can go to McDonald's for lunch?

Once on your vacation, keep a running tally of what you spend each day for each area of expense. Making adjustments while on the trip will help you come in below or on target. If you truly overestimated and have some money left, spend it on the vacation as a last-minute treat. If you think this seems too tedious, recall the shock when the credit-card statement arrived after your last vacation.

However you pay—cash, traveler's checks, or credit card—keep the total running. Don't carry all your funds in cash, and for safety's sake, split what cash you do carry between adults.

Saving for Your First Home

Owning a home is the American dream. Most of us don't want to live in a house that belongs to someone else. That desire has driven a lot of people into buying before they were ready financially.

But, remember, owning is not always preferable to renting. Where I live, rent for a modest home is two hundred to three hundred dollars more a month than a mortgage payment. Buying makes sense in this environment. On the other hand, I have a business colleague who lives where he can rent for a reasonable monthly amount. He rented one house for eight years and recently rented another he expects to be in for several years. By renting he saves a big down payment. If the houses in your area are not appreciating quickly and you expect to have to move in less than three years, it probably isn't a good idea to buy. You would lose money after paying a Realtor's commission and the other costs of selling.

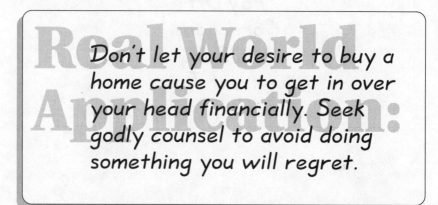

Don't let your desire to buy a home cause you to get in over your head financially. Seek godly counsel to avoid doing something you will regret.

For example, suppose you bought a house that cost $100,000, and it appreciated in value by only 2 percent a year. It would be worth a little over $106,000 in three years. After the Realtor's commission of 6 percent taking about $6,300, and other selling expenses of $1,000, you would net $98,700 and lose $1,300.

Ideally you should save 10 to 20 percent for a down payment for your first house. (The Federal Housing Administration has a program permitting qualified homebuyers to buy a house with little down payment, but your interest will be slightly higher on an FHA loan.)

Trying to save from regular monthly cash flow for a down payment is tough. Young families trying to make ends meet are usually strapped with payments on credit cards and car loans. Heavy monthly debt service may mean paying off debts before saving can begin. But begin to save as soon as possible, even if it is just a little. It is much easier to increase what you are saving than to start saving. Even if you can only afford to save ten dollars a month at first, start with that. Can you take on extra jobs and put the earnings toward the down payment? Although it may seem like an impossible goal, begin to save. Pray for God's provision, and be diligent.

ACTION
STEP 6:
*Pay Off
Car Loans
and Save
for Next Time*

8
- - - - - - - - - -
Don't Laugh, It's Paid For

READ THE AD and what does it say? "Low monthly payments." This new car payment isn't just low, it's *really* low.

The temptation is great, isn't it? Shopping for a new car is an American pastime. When we read ads that say, "Walk in, drive out with a new car; no hassle," we want to believe it. If we still owe on our car, the copy that reads, "Let us pay off what's left of the loan on your trade-in car," is all too inviting. Even though we were always told to read the fine print carefully, wandering into a car dealership may prove to be our downfall. Only later, after the new-car smell has worn off, do we begin to realize that the offer was too good to be true.

Some of us may take a high car payment for granted. It's part of the budget we plan to live with the rest of our lives. But it doesn't have to be that way. Take a step back and examine whether your new-car rationale needs changing.

BUYING A USED CAR INSTEAD OF NEW

As you know, I come from the original buy-a-new-car school. I thought it was more cost effective to buy new and trade every three or four years. I also believed the Detroit rumor that keeping a car with over fifty thousand miles on the odometer was asking for trouble. But when Elizabeth and I started having financial troubles, we found we couldn't make the payment even with a trade-in. At one point we sold one car to get out of the payment and bought an older car with cash. I made this move out of necessity, not as a well-thought-out decision.

As I drive my older cars longer and longer, I have found that they don't fall to pieces after fifty thousand miles, or even after one hundred thousand miles. By keeping them well maintained, I get a lot more service than I ever thought possible.

My colleague, Jim Underwood, has used the same approach for many years. He buys a used car only after a thorough mechanical inspection. His "new" cars are detailed, even to the point of a new coat of paint. His wife, Mary Anne, drives the eleven-year-old car, while Jim drives the thirteen-year-old car. Jim carefully maintains his cars, and each car is detailed once a year, giving it a new-car feel and luster. Jim and Mary Anne can afford new cars, but they choose to spend their resources in other ways.

We aren't saying this approach is for everyone. God has given one of my clients a high income. Though he drives new cars, his kingdom giving is well over a tithe. The more money he makes, the higher the percentage of income he gives each year. But if you're a middle-income American without a six-figure income, I would ask you to stop and think through whether you should approach car buying differently.

I must admit that I haven't been delivered from my yearning for new cars. But God has shown me that on my own I would still rationalize the need for a new car, when economically it doesn't make as much sense as driving the cars I have. As financial counselor Ron Blue says, "The cheapest car you can ever own is the one you are driving right now."

Even though I advocate buying and driving used cars, I am not an advocate of the old clunker theory. At some point it is no longer practical to continue driving a used car. However, I continue to discover that the time to get rid of a car is much later than I first thought.

Make transportation plans seeking God's wisdom. Put achieving those plans in God's hands. We may set a timetable that can't be met.

> *Make transportation plans seeking God's wisdom. Put achieving those plans in God's hands. We may set a timetable that can't be met. The plan may not necessarily be bad; more time may be required for fulfillment.*

The plan may not necessarily be bad; more time may be required for fulfillment.

I had to learn in some hard ways that God is in control. I can make plans, but only God can make them happen. My plan may be good, but my timing is not God's timing.

How does this approach work out in real life? I can't think of a better example than my family's van. We bought it used. It had all the features we wanted, but we didn't do our homework on the reliability of this model. That van was nothing but trouble. I calculated in frustration that we had put $2,000 into it the first year. I hoped we had replaced or repaired everything, but it never stopped. At the end of four years we had spent $7,000 in repairs, which comes to over $140 a month—well over the average of $50 to $100 per month, but much less than a new car payment. Every time I looked at new car ads, I realized the payments would be over $300 a month, and the van was costing much less each year.

I finally resigned myself to buying another used van, and I picked up one of those free cars-for-sale magazines. I read through it but decided to wait another six months. The next day during my early morning walk, I was thanking God for keeping me from making another car mistake when I thought back to one particular ad. When I got home, I had another look at the ad and thought it had possibilities. When I showed it to Elizabeth she said, "Why don't you check it out?"

I called the owner, George Miller, and he was willing to meet us halfway at an interstate exit. Now I was really nervous. Elizabeth and I were both praying that God would stop the deal from going through if it wasn't from him.

As it turned out, George had just lost his job and could not continue making his payments, so he was planning to buy something older and less expensive. He had found a new job, but the pay was considerably less than what he had been earning. The price he was asking was reasonable and the van was many miles and years younger than ours. The captain's chairs behind the front bucket seats were on our wish list, the air conditioning was cold, the tires looked new. Cosmetically, the vehicle was in mint condition. Our family wanted it, but I couldn't begin to talk seriously without an under-the-hood inspection. We agreed to have a mechanic run a test. The van checked out with flying colors.

George and I talked on the phone. He didn't want to give up the van and had always taken loving care of it, changing the oil himself every three thousand miles. Then he asked me, "What are you going to do with your van?" George suggested a trade. I had already told him about our van's problems, but he didn't seem to mind. We ended up going to his bank and paying off his balance. We exchanged vans. Both of us were happy.

I believe God protected us and answered our prayers. We now have a "new" van which we enjoy immensely. It has features I could never have justified if we had bought new. We owe a little money on it, but we should have that paid off in twelve to thirteen months. With God's help, we are moving to where we need to be: out of the red, into the black, especially with our cars.

SAVING TO BUY A CAR

Most people ask, "How much car can I buy for the monthly payment I can afford?" Suppose Mark and Paula Robinson trade in their Honda Accord and borrow to buy a new car. Based on the following numbers, let's calculate their monthly payment:

Cost of new car	$18,000
Subtract value of trade-in	– 4,000
Amount to finance	$14,000
Finance period	48 months
Interest rate	10%
Monthly payment	$355.08

Suppose instead of borrowing to pay for the car, they save enough over forty-eight months to pay for it with cash, and earn a return on their savings of 5 percent. How much would they have to set aside each month to have the cash difference of fourteen thousand dollars?

Amount needed	$14,000
Time available to save	48 months
Return on savings	5%
Monthly savings for new car	$264.08

If they save to buy the car with cash instead of financing, they will need to set aside only $264.08 a month, instead of financing at $355.08 each month. It would cost them $91.00 a month less if they save first, which is $1,092 per year, or $4,368 over four years. This

How do you begin saving for a car when you still have payments on the car you have now? The secret is to finance your car for four years, drive it for eight, and keep setting aside the amount of your monthly car payment after it's paid off.

savings is why we should all have the goal to save and pay for our next car with cash. And if the Robinsons take that $91.00 a month and save it over twenty years earning 10 percent, the total will grow to over $69,000.

You may be thinking, How do I begin saving for a car when I still have payments on the car I have now? The secret is to finance your car for four years, drive it for eight, and keep setting aside the amount of your monthly car payment after it's paid. Eventually, you will become your own banker, giving yourself an interest-free loan.

I realize this approach isn't always possible. If you are unable to save enough to pay for your next car with cash, save as much as you can for a down payment and finance the difference for as short a period as possible. When your car is paid for, continue to set aside the payment to pay cash for its replacement. Once we begin to save and to pay cash for cars and drive them for six or eight years instead of three or four, we will have more time to save for the next one, and we can reduce significantly the monthly amount we must set aside for replacement.

Let's consider the Robinsons again. Instead of driving a car and trading it in after four years, suppose they drive it twice as long and trade it in after eight years. The Robinsons would have ninety-six months to save for their next car, instead of only forty-eight. If

> *If you can't save enough to pay for your next car with cash, save as much as you can and borrow the rest for as large a monthly payment as you can afford for the shortest period. Then save to pay cash next time.*

Real World Application:

they need $14,000 cash plus their trade-in and can earn 5 percent interest, then they would have to set aside only $118.91 per month instead of the $264.08 they'd set aside over four years. This is a reduction of another $145.17 per month in the amount required to purchase a car. By driving a car eight years instead of four, and saving to pay cash instead of borrowing, the amount the Robinsons need to pay monthly for their car purchase can be reduced from   08 to $118.91 per month. That reduces the monthly am   bout a third of the previous amount, freeing a lot of m   year to meet other goals. And, if the Robinsons invest the   monthly reduction in car payments with a 10 percent return   r twenty years, the accumulated savings would surpass $179,000.

Of course, over several years the cost of a car is going to increase, and the $18,000 car today may cost $26,000 eight years from now. If we assume a 6 percent increase in the cost of cars every year, the simplest way to handle it is to increase each year the amount we set aside by double the inflation rate, or 12 percent. In other words, if we set aside $118.91 per month this year, next year we would increase the amount to $133.18 ($118.91 x 1.12). The following year we would increase the amount to $149.16 ($133.18 x 1.12), and so on. This will not give us the exact amount needed, but it will be close enough.

While working your way toward buying with cash, you might have to borrow a little. If so, shop for the best deal. Sometimes dealers can give you the best interest and the best terms. But it doesn't hurt to check with your bank or credit union. You might even check with someone you've never dealt with financially. Knowing you are shopping might cause a dealer to sweeten the terms. Even if a dealer comes down or gives you better terms, get another quote or two. Ask the dealer for a better deal on financing.

Think about other sources of funding if you haven't saved all you need. Borrow from yourself if you have all or part of what you need in a life insurance policy. If you have equity in your home, consider a home equity loan, which is normally at a lower interest rate than car loans. Plus, you can deduct the interest you pay. Be careful with home equity loans. Don't let the lender convince you to borrow more than necessary.

HOW TO BUY A USED CAR

Buying a used car is like walking in the dark for most of us. I agree that buying a used car is riskier than buying a new car, but it is the best way to come out ahead, and many of the pitfalls can be avoided.

1. *Determine your needs.*

    Decide what you need in a car before you start ~~looking~~. Do you need a minivan, or can you get by with a st~~ation wagon~~? Do you need a large car, or will a smaller one th~~at's cheaper~~ to operate meet your needs? What features do ~~you need~~? Automatic transmission or manual? List essential features.

2. *Decide what you can spend.*

    Then pick up a copy of an autos-for-sale magazine at your neighborhood convenience store and get a feel for car prices. Go to the library and find out the retail and loan value of cars you are interested in. Cars two to three years old are the best buy because most of the resale value is lost during those first years.

3. *If you're going to finance, check around for the best interest rates.*

    Find out if the lender will finance a car the age you're considering. How much cash will you need for a down payment?

4. *If you're considering particular models, check their reputation.*

    Ask people who own them if they've been pleased with their performance. If you know a mechanic, ask him. You can also check the surveys auto magazines conduct.

5. *Pray.*

    Ask God to lead you to a reliable car with the right price, then start looking. Tell people you're looking. Call about the cars in auto-sale magazines. Try the used car lot of new car dealers. (I prefer these over used car dealers because new car dealers are more concerned about their reputation.)

6. *Test drive it.*

    After you've found a car you're interested in, drive it on the highway at cruising speed and around town. Ask questions. If anything seems wrong with the car, take a knowledgeable friend back with you to look at it. If everything seems to check

out, take it to a mechanic for a thorough inspection. If anything needs repair, ask for a repair estimate. This estimate
becomes a bargaining tool to justify a lower offer.

7. *Get away to pray before you decide.*

   If you don't have peace about the car, don't buy it. You
   may pass up what seems like a good deal, but it isn't worth
   the risk. If you sense God's peace and everything checks out,
   make an offer. If you can pay cash and you're buying from
   an owner who can't provide financing or take a trade-in, you
   probably can offer less. Your cash is a bargaining tool.

8. *Sell your old car yourself.*

   Experts agree this is the best way to get the most money
   for your car. If you think this is a hassle, remember that trading it in can lose you up to two to three thousand dollars.

Preventive Maintenance for Your Car

Whether you buy a new or used car, take care of it. Remember
some basic tips to save on repairs:

1. Find a reliable, honest, independent mechanic and stick with
   him. Follow whatever maintenance plan he suggests. The service department at a dealership has more overhead and will
   need to charge more.
2. Wash and wax the car regularly and keep the interior clean.
3. Fix any problems before they get worse and costlier.
4. Don't drive with dirty (worn out) oil. Change your oil every
   three months or every three thousand miles, whichever comes
   first. If the level is a quart low, your oil probably needs changing. Follow the owner's manual, but remember that 10W30
   protects the engine better than 10W40 in most cases. Don't fall
   into the trap of using oil additives. Just change the oil often to
   reduce engine wear.
5. Watch out for dirty gas. Fuel filters need changing every two
   years or ten thousand miles, whichever comes last. Clogged filters and sludge in gas lines impair a car's fuel efficiency and
   cause stalling or failure to start.

6. Follow the book. An owner's manual lists what maintenance to perform when. Power-steering fluid needs a change every thirty thousand miles or three years, whichever comes first. The manual doesn't always say, but brake fluid needs replacement every twenty-four thousand miles or two years, whichever comes first. Timing chains may require replacement at one hundred thousand miles, timing belts every sixty thousand miles.

7. We don't have this problem in Florida, but up north, turn on your air conditioner every couple of weeks. Do the same for the defroster. Your emergency brake should be engaged frequently, even daily.

8. Anti-freeze should be changed every two years or twenty-four thousand miles to prevent rust buildup. Use a fifty-fifty mix of anti-freeze and distilled water, even in hot climates.

9. Poorly charged batteries can weaken an alternator or starter. Batteries are cheaper to replace, so keep them charged and buy a new one before the warranty ends.

10. If you live where it's hot, protect the car's interior by putting a sun protector in the windshield when your car is parked.

11. Don't drive with sudden starts and stops. You won't reach your destination faster by racing away from a stoplight and braking hard for the next red light. What you will speed up is gasoline consumption and wear on your engine, transmission, brakes, and suspension.

12. If you travel in mountains, downshift on steep grades, but don't overdo it. Better to replace brakes than repair an engine or transmission.

13. Start the car without pushing hard on the accelerator. Let the car warm up for a minute before starting to drive. Your car's bearings and head gaskets will benefit from tender care.

14. Most people know a manual transmission costs less to keep up than an automatic. But that's only true if you shift properly. Keep a gear running between two and three thousand RPM. Don't leave your foot on the clutch or your hand on the gearshift. If you hear a grinding noise while shifting from neutral to first gear, shift from neutral to second briefly, then back to first. Use overdrive only if traveling forty-five miles per hour or more.

LEASING A CAR

Many Americans are turning to the lease option. Lower monthly payments and little down are strong reasons car dealers offer to sell you a lease. And people like the fact that they don't have thousands of dollars tied up in a car and can return it before all the newness has worn off. But we normally recommend purchasing over leasing because in most instances purchasing is a better deal. It allows us to drive cars longer and reduce the monthly cost.

Watch out for pitfalls when leasing. If you think purchase advertising can be confusing, you haven't started reading lease ads. Ambiguity abounds, and consequently, more states are passing truth-in-leasing laws. When *60 Minutes* did an expose of rampant deception in leasing ads, even many CPAs had trouble making out the fine print. Comparative shopping is difficult with a lease because you have to break out the true cost of the car, the interest rate (money factor), and the residual value (worth of the car at the end of the lease). Offers continue to change and become more confusing, but in rare instances a manufacturer may put some of its own money into a lease to help get rid of a slow-moving model.

Another negative aspect is that you are locked into the terms of the lease, and at the end you own nothing. You cannot get out of most leases without a substantial penalty, if at all. Even if you like the car and want to keep it, you must purchase the remaining value. The longer the lease, the more interest you pay. If you drive a lot, you may put on more miles than the lease allows and be charged a penalty of ten to fifteen cents per mile. You also could be charged for excessive wear and tear.

If you believe you must lease, shop around just as you would when borrowing money to purchase a car. Find a financially astute friend to help you read all the fine print, and compare leasing contracts from more than one source. Whatever you do, make sure there are no verbal agreements. Anything "guaranteed" must be written into the contract.

So many emotional factors are involved in obtaining transportation. Before you make any move, wait and pray. Ask the Lord what he wants you to drive and how to pay for your next vehicle.

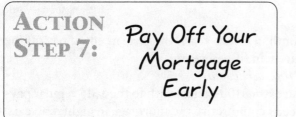

Pay Off Your Mortgage Early

9

Paying for the Castle

EVERYONE WANTS to own a home and all of us would like to pay off our mortgage quickly. Consider Micah and Betsy Green. They live on Micah's $42,000 salary as a banker because Betsy works at home, taking care of their nearly one-year-old daughter. The Greens live in a twenty-year-old red brick house in a nice neighborhood with nice neighbors. They like the mix of older and younger families.

The house cost $86,500 and the Greens financed $80,000 at 8.5 percent for thirty years. When they sought help, they were only making the monthly payment of $615 (excluding taxes and insurance). We zeroed in on this large budget item. With an amortization schedule we reviewed ways to pay off the house more quickly and save a bundle in interest charges.

Here were the three options we considered:

1. *Refinance.*
   Interest rates were lower, so the Greens could obtain a mortgage at 8 percent for fifteen years. Monthly payments would increase to $764.
2. *Pay extra principal each month.*
   While the principal goes up each month, it doesn't become dramatically higher until year eleven. By making the regular $615 payment, adding about $48 a month the first year, and

more each month in future years, the Greens could pay off the mortgage entirely in fifteen years.

3. *Pay an extra $100 each month.*

By adding an extra $100 each month to the $615 regular payment, the Greens could retire the mortgage in eighteen years.

The Greens chose option 2, but with a twist. They decided to make an extra principal payment each month for three years while they were getting rid of their consumer debt. Once that was down to zero, they moved to option 1 and refinanced at 8 percent for fifteen years. They were able to save $84,000 in interest and the new payments on a fifteen-year mortgage were lower than if they had gone with option 1 originally.

As we've seen in the case of credit cards, you can't go wrong with prepayment, especially on what is probably the single largest debt item in your budget.

We live in uncertain economic times. We can expect to change jobs more frequently than in past generations. Changing jobs today is not always our decision to make. Re-engineering has left job security in question, even with the most stable companies. Estimates abound that in the years ahead, more of us will be self-employed, resulting in more erratic income streams.

After you read this chapter, coordinate your mortgage payoff strategy with the action step in the next chapter—saving for an emergency. The steps go together, especially in an unstable economy.

Let's consider what's best for you if you don't have a home, or if you are preparing to find a new mortgage because you recently moved. Then we'll look at options if you are currently paying on a mortgage.

SAVING ON A MORTGAGE BEFORE YOU SIGN UP

As in borrowing money for a car, it never hurts to shop. If you are looking for your first mortgage, watch for special bond arrangements that offer lower interest rates to first-time buyers. If you are in the military or are a veteran, VA loans are available at good rates with no money down. Hard to find but worth searching for are people selling their home with an assumable mortgage at a 1950s rate of three or four percent. Oh, for the good old days.

Here are some other hints that can save you money before you sign on the dotted line:

- Interest rates normally aren't negotiable but points are. Your financial institution wants all your business. If it knows you are shopping, it may be willing to drop the points.
- Ask for document preparation fees to be waived.
- Fewer lenders are charging attorneys' fees, but if they show up, say you would rather not pay the lender's attorney bill.
- Adjustable-rate mortgages go up and down in popularity. If you are taking an ARM because you can't afford to buy the house any other way, don't buy. You really are not in the ballpark to buy a house. The only reason to take out an ARM is if you are certain you won't be living in the house more than a few years. If you are confident of trading up in three years or know your company will move you soon, the cheapest ARM you can find makes sense. But your situation can change, so this is still a risk.
- Try as hard as possible to make a 20 percent down payment so you won't be required to buy private mortgage insurance. That can add .3 percent to .66 percent to your monthly payment on a thirty-year fixed-rate mortgage. If you can only come up with less than 20 percent and are forced to take private mortgage insurance, remember, you don't have to pay it forever.

REFINANCING A MORTGAGE

Refinancing may make sense for you, but before you sign on the dotted line, ask a lot of questions. There's more than one reason to refinance or not refinance:

- First and foremost, people go after new mortgages when interest rates dive and refinancing would drop their payments hundreds of dollars a month. This is a great deal, especially if it doesn't take long to pay back the refinancing expenses. The hundreds saved were already in their budget and can be applied to paying extra principal each month.

- If you've exhausted all other means to finance a college education, you might want to take equity out of a home you've owned for several years. But be careful and don't overdo it. A tax-deductible home equity loan or credit line might be more appropriate than refinancing.
- If your adjustable rate mortgage is getting ready to take an interest hike, or if interest rates just dropped, now is probably the time to switch to a conventional loan.

The main question to ask is how long it will take for the savings switch expenses to catch up with your current payment. If it's going to take several years, reconsider. Don't stop after asking about the new payment. Find out all one-time costs, such as attorneys' fees (yours and theirs), appraisal fees, title insurance and search fees, application fee, credit check, inspections, taxes, transfer fees, and points.

Just as in taking out a first mortgage it pays to let your current mortgage holder know you are shopping. Obtain quotations over the phone; don't use lunch hours for the next week to make personal visits.

If interest rates have dropped 5 percent below what you are now paying but you don't have the money for closing costs, consider taking out a loan or asking the new lender to finance the closing. Even better, ask the lender to pay for the closing expenses.

If the lender finances the closing costs, take the resulting savings in monthly payments and pay that amount against the mortgage principal until you have paid the equivalent of the closing costs. For example, suppose you have determined that your monthly mortgage payment will go down by $100 a month after you refinance, but the closing costs for refinancing are $2400. After you have your new mortgage, take the $100 monthly reduction in your mortgage payment and pay it toward your principal until you have reduced the mortgage balance by the $2400 added closing costs. The reason? If you don't do this, you may be financing the closing costs over thirty years and paying several thousand dollars more in interest on the $2400. You may gain in the short run, but it will cost you dearly in the long run.

Also, when you refinance, consider getting a shorter mortgage period. Otherwise, you are putting back your time to pay off your house to thirty years after reducing it by several years. When we decided to refinance several years ago, we had twenty-five years left on our mortgage. The thought of exchanging our remaining twenty-five years for a thirty-year mortgage was unsettling, so I asked if we could set up the refinanced mortgage on a twenty-five year schedule, and the lender agreed.

But you may be thinking, We won't be living in this house longer than just a few more years, so it doesn't matter if the mortgage pay-off time goes back to thirty years. There are two problems with this rationale. First, the longer the mortgage period, the smaller the percentage of your monthly payment applied to principal. Whether you keep your house thirty years or sell it after a few more years, having a smaller mortgage balance at any time along the way is obviously better. Second, we never really know what the future holds. We have now been in our home for eight and one-half years. We originally expected to sell it after three years.

One potential problem is that you can refinance only 80 percent of the home's appraised value for a conventional mortgage. If you started out with a low down payment and have owned the house for a short time, you might be disqualified.

When is the timing right? Just as you never know when a stock has reached its highest value, you will never know when interest rates have bottomed out. So don't continue to lose hundreds of dollars as you wait to see if rates will keep dropping. If you qualify for refinancing and can find a good deal with a short time to pay off expenses, do it now.

Let's consider ways to prepay, and you can decide what's best.

Mortgage Prepayment Strategies

Strategy 1

Take money available after paying off credit-card and other consumer debt and put it toward mortgage principal.

Mark and Paula Robinson have a mortgage payment of $697, an interest rate of 8 percent, and a balance of $95,000. If they pay off their Visa card and Discover card with a monthly payment of $100 combined, and their First National education loan with a monthly payment of $89 (see fig. 2), they would gain $189 per month to speed up paying off their mortgage principal. They could retire their thirty-year mortgage in fifteen years and save $82,000 in interest.

Even an additional $75 per month can make a big difference in the length of the mortgage. Suppose instead of $189, the Robinsons pay $75 per month toward mortgage principal with their regular payment. The life of the loan would go down from thirty to twenty-one years. Interest savings would be an impressive $51,000.

Strategy 2

Make the next principal payment with each mortgage payment.

In the early stages of a mortgage, the portion of the monthly payment that reduces principal can be very small, as seen in the amortization schedule below. The Robinsons have a thirty-year $95,000 mortgage with an interest rate of 8 percent. Their monthly payments are $697.00. As you can see from their amortization schedule, $633.33 of the first payment will go toward interest and a mere $63.74 for principal. In their second month's payment, the amount going to principal increases to only $64.17. So the portion of a payment applied to principal gradually rises each month.

Payment Number	Payment Amount	Interest Portion	Principal Portion	Remaining Balance
1	$697.00	$633.33	$63.74	$94,936.00
2	$697.00	$632.91	$64.17	$94,872.00
3	$697.00	$632.48	$64.60	$94,807.00
4	$697.00	$632.05	$65.02	$94,742.00

Using strategy 2, the Robinsons would make the next principal payment with each monthly payment. With their first payment of $697.00, they would pay the second principal payment of $64.17. Their next payment of $697.00 would be treated as payment 3, and with it they would pay the fourth principal payment of $65.02. Their next payment of $697.00 would become payment 5, and they would pay principal payment 6. If they continued making the next principal payment with each mortgage payment, the extra principal payment would gradually increase each month and their mortgage would be paid off in fifteen years instead of thirty, saving more than $82,000 in interest.

Strategy 3

Make mortgage payments every four weeks instead of each month.

For people who are paid every week or every two weeks instead of monthly, paying the mortgage every four weeks is a strategy worth considering. With thirteen four-week periods in a year, you will end up making an extra month's payment each year. It's important to be sure the thirteenth payment is paid only toward principal. The Robinsons' mortgage could be paid off in about twenty-two years instead of thirty with this approach.

The key is finding a strategy that fits your budget, is easy to do, and that you will consistently apply. Choose a prepayment approach, stick with it, and watch it work.

A common approach that comes close to the thirteenth monthly payment each year outlined in strategy 3 is to divide your mortgage into a biweekly payment. Paying biweekly can reduce a thirty-year mortgage to eighteen to twenty-two years, depending on the interest rate. I'm including this not as a separate strategy but to provide some necessary background.

Most bankers will not sell you a biweekly mortgage. The few who do may charge a higher interest rate. Multilevel marketing approaches

Real World Application:

Choose a prepayment approach, stick with it, and watch it work.

and other private companies promise to turn your mortgage into a biweekly. Beware. Promises are not always as good as they sound. There's usually a healthy setup charge and then ongoing transaction fees each time you send your biweekly payment. Some companies draft your checking account for your biweekly payment but send only one or two extra principal payments each year to the mortgage company.

If biweekly sounds good, why not do it yourself? Don't pay anyone for this service. If your monthly mortgage is $1,200, divide by twelve and pay that extra amount on principal each month. The $1,200, plus $100 for extra principal, will give you just about the same saving as buying into the offer of a biweekly company. And you save the setup and extra charges.

Other Ideas

To explore more ways of prepaying a mortgage, purchase Marc Eisenson's classic book, *The Banker's Secret* (see appendix E). Eisenson also publishes a newsletter showing how to get out of debt, often sharing readers' success stories, sells a computer software program, and answers a hotline phone number. Eisenson recommends you start with the loose change approach to mortgage prepayment. Accumulate loose change from your pocket every night for the month, and put that toward mortgage principal.

One family pays its ten-year-old son to count and roll spare change, allowing him to keep anything more than twenty-five dollars. The twenty-five dollars is applied monthly to the family's $40,000 mortgage. Another couple decided to cut their cigarette intake by half and with the savings will subtract eleven years from their mortgage, not to mention adding a few years to their lives. Most personal money management software programs allow you to print out amortization schedules. If you want a schedule for various mortgage amounts with different terms and interest amounts, larger bookstores carry mortgage tables books.

REASONS NOT TO PREPAY A MORTGAGE

You may have noticed we don't approach finances with ironclad rules. Everyone's circumstances are different. We use guiding principles from Scripture, coupled with common sense. So sometimes there are reasons for you not to prepay a mortgage. Along with reviewing the issue logically, we challenge our counseling clients to make the decision a matter of prayer.

Are there certain kinds of loans I shouldn't prepay?

The answer here is a resounding yes! More and more states have outlawed the practice, but if you are holding a mortgage using the Rule of 78s, prepaying can result in penalties. Some consumer loans also use the Rule of 78s, which is a way to front-load interest rates. Even refinancing doesn't always make sense for a Rule of 78s loan. This is a complicated approach to lending money, one I won't even try to explain. But if you have such a loan, you are probably better off if you invest extra money and let this loan go to the end. Then, never again enter into such a transaction.

Should I hold off prepayment because of losing the tax deduction?

You will hear many suggestions. Your brother-in-law may say prepaying is foolish because you will lose the tax deductions. This sounds sensible, but let's consider the theory.

If you are married, the standard deduction for joint filing in 1996 was $6,700. Suppose your itemized deductions are $9,000, including $5,500 in mortgage interest. If your mortgage were paid off, you would lose the $5,500 house deduction. But then you could take the standard deduction of $6,700.

Suppose you are in the 33 percent tax bracket, your mortgage interest paid in one year is $8,000, and other itemized deductions total $7,800. With total deductions of $15,800, paying off the mortgage would reduce the tax deduction by the full amount of interest paid, since the other itemized deductions are greater than the standard deduction. In non-accounting language, do you want to pay $8,000 in interest to save $2,640 in taxes? I wouldn't think so. Keeping a mortgage strictly for the tax deduction rarely makes economic sense. The one exception is pastors who are paid housing allowances. Ask an accountant to explain why.

Should I invest money at a higher interest rate and then pay off the mortgage in one lump sum?

You can find higher rates of return than the amount you are paying on your mortgage, but not without risks. For most people holding mortgages in the 7 to 8 percent range, there are a number of fairly good medium-risk mutual funds returning around 10 percent. On paper, it seems to make sense to keep an 8 percent mortgage and invest available money in mutual funds with 10 percent or greater return. But you should consider two things when trying to decide whether to put invested money toward mortgage reduction. First, the mortgage interest rate is guaranteed; mutual fund returns are not. Second, your decision is not strictly financial.

Remember in strategy 1 that the Robinsons could pay off their thirty-year mortgage in fifteen years if they paid their monthly payment of $697 and added $189 in extra principal? If they invested this $189 instead and could earn 8 percent, after taxes, they would have enough in approximately sixteen years to pay off their mortgage in a lump sum. So investing the funds and paying off the mortgage at one time accomplishes the same result as following strategy 1.

I prefer investing the funds and paying off the mortgage all at one time. My reason is the flexibility this offers for some unforeseen circumstance. I'm not talking about taking the money out after finding a good deal on the bass boat you've always wanted. No, I'm talking about being seven years into prepaying a mortgage when you suddenly are out of a job and find it takes six months to land another. Or suppose your boss says in order to keep the plant open everyone from the president to the janitor must take a 40 percent pay cut starting next month. The company believes this will keep the factory afloat but can make no promise when full salaries, much less pending raises, will resume. Such crises could put your mortgage payoff in jeopardy. No matter how much extra you paid toward your mortgage principal, you could still lose the house and the built-up equity. The extra paid toward mortgage principal comes off the back end of the loan and doesn't permit us to skip some payments.

Sometimes a client will say, "The bank would never do that after I have made all of those extra payments." Others say, "I should be able to keep up my payments somehow if that happened." Although either statement may prove true, the wise home owner doesn't count on it. Again, I prefer staying flexible. If the worst happens, you could use the funds in your investments to carry you through the difficulties without risking your home.

How do I invest if I choose to not prepay but instead save to pay off my mortgage?

If you decide to invest funds and pay off your mortgage with a single check, you need a resource for investing that provides a return after taxes greater than your mortgage interest rate. The Robinsons need a return higher than 8 percent without taking an unnecessary risk. With a tax rate of 33 percent, the Robinsons need a return of 12 percent or more before taxes. Over the last ten to fifteen years a number of well-managed mutual funds have earned this kind of return.

One source for investing is the discount broker, Charles Schwab and Company. Its brokers are salaried, not commissioned, so they can recommend investments that best suit your needs without steering you to those paying the broker the highest commission. They also sell no-load (no commission) mutual funds, which are especially good if you are not planning to stay in a fund for the next twenty years. Schwab offices offer easy-to-read booklets on investing, and the company conducts frequent seminars. (See appendix E on how to contact this firm.)

If you want to spend more time with your investments, another source is the *Sound Mind Investing* newsletter, published by Austin Pryor. Pryor writes for Larry Burkett's newsletter and has been a guest on Burkett's radio program. He has also written the book *Sound Mind Investing* (published by Moody Press), a good source of investment principles. His newsletter recommends specific mutual funds for investing. (See appendix E for the telephone number and address to obtain a free copy.)

A third source is Atlanta-based Ron Blue and Company, which has offices around the country. People who have accumulated at least $25,000 can use this organization to make their investments. The company works for a fee only and is attractive to people who don't want daily contact with their investments. Appendix E contains a number of publications we recommend for you to become more knowledgeable before you begin to invest outside of a local savings account.

Should I invest money in a retirement plan instead of using that money to pay off my mortgage?

If you are eligible to participate in a retirement plan through your employer, and your employer matches your contributions, it may be better to put available funds toward your retirement plan rather than paying off your mortgage.

A dollar-for-dollar match by your employer is equivalent to an instant 100 percent return. An employer contribution of fifty cents for each of your dollars is equivalent to an instant 50 percent return. Although there are restrictions on the availability of the funds, this kind of return is too great to ignore. Some retirement plans allow you to borrow and then repay the money over time. You may be able to borrow to pay off your mortgage, or to finance a college education. These are untaxed dollars when you put them in and while they are compounding in your retirement account. In some plans, taxes are due only when you withdraw funds other than through the borrowing plan.

If your retirement plan is in financial difficulty, you probably should pass on investing your money to take advantage of the employer match. The employer matching program is of little value if you will never receive the funds because the retirement plan goes bankrupt. If you think there is some question about the solvency of your employer's plan, consider asking a CPA or "fee only" financial advisor to review details of the plan and give you an opinion.

Should I prepay my mortgage or save for my children's college education?

If you have children who will be college age before you can pay off your mortgage, you should consider delaying acceleration of a mortgage payoff and invest funds for college instead.

Action Step 9 in a later chapter will cover saving for your children's higher education. If your children don't go to college, the saved funds could be used to pay off the mortgage.

If your employer matches your retirement plan contributions, consider putting available funds in your retirement plan instead of accelerating your mortgage payoff. What your employer matches is an instant return.

Build
an Emergency
Reserve for Life's
Surprises

10
- - - - - - - - - - -

Hit from Behind

AS PRIME MINISTER of Egypt,
Joseph had great responsibilities. Pharaoh was the highest figurehead,
but keeping the country running smoothly was Joseph's job. In a
dream, he learned there would be seven years of plenty followed by
seven years of famine. Because he set the nation on a course of saving,
Egypt survived the lean times and even had extra to share with outsiders, including Joseph's family (Genesis 41–45).

You and I don't know when the next famine will appear in our
lives, but one is likely at some point. To make it through a drought,
we must have money set aside. The Book of Proverbs is chock-full
of advice to be prepared.

> "A prudent man foresees the difficulties ahead and prepares for
> them; the simpleton goes blindly on and suffers the conse-
> quences" (Prov. 22:3 LB).
> "The wise man looks ahead. The fool attempts to fool himself and
> won't face facts" (Prov. 14:8 LB).
> "The wise man saves for the future, but the foolish man spends
> whatever he gets" (Prov. 21:20 LB).

An emergency reserve can reduce the impact of an unexpected
need. Most financial planners recommend the average household

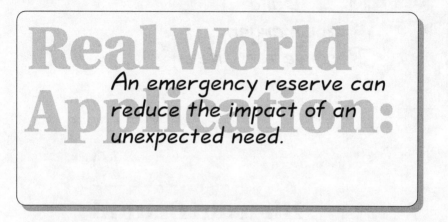

Real World Application:

An emergency reserve can reduce the impact of an unexpected need.

keep three to six months' net income in reserve. If several thousand dollars were accumulated while completing the previous steps outlined, an additional cash reserve this large should not be necessary. A reserve equal to two months' take-home pay should be adequate, and if a large unexpected financial need occurs that exhausts the two-month reserve, the other accumulated funds serve as a backup.

There is a danger in having an emergency cash reserve. Once we've accumulated the funds, we might begin to trust in them rather than in God. I suspect one reason God has allowed financial calamities to occur in my household is to remind me that he is the ultimate provider who meets all our needs. It is God who gives the opportunity to accumulate the funds for true emergencies.

We should also be ready to give to others out of our emergency funds. How many times have you experienced God placing a giving opportunity on your heart but lacked the money to give? Be sensitive to these opportunities, and pray about using some of the emergency funds. Ability to give above a tithe is a real privilege and a source of great joy. Be careful with this if you are susceptible to emotional appeals for money. Make sure God is in your desire by waiting before giving.

WHAT IS A TRUE EMERGENCY?

When we start to save money, we need to spell out the objectives. Saving for no purpose is hoarding, which is despised by God. Money accumulated in this life will rot away. Our most expensive clothes eventually will become moth-eaten. James writes in chapter 5 to warn those who live in self-indulgence. You also remember the story Christ told of the rich, egotistical farmer who enjoyed planning how to hoard more grain by building bigger barns. Our Lord's ominous words were that this man's life would be required that very night (see Luke 12).

Saving out of fear for the future is evidence of a lack of faith in God's provision. Worry was addressed head-on by Jesus in Matthew 6:25–34. None of the rest of creation worries; why should we? The theme Christ provides is that we are safe in the hands of our heavenly Father, so there need be no place in our hearts for anxiety about the future. Saving should ride in tandem with seeking first the kingdom of God. When saving, we must be sure to seek God's direction through prayer to avoid improper motives.

Our objective is to save for emergencies that would hinder our kingdom service. Emergencies could mean:

1. Losing a job and lacking funds to cover basic living expenses for a time.
2. Becoming ill or having surgery and being without a paycheck for an unknown time.
3. Incurring significant medical expenses not covered by health insurance.
4. Experiencing an unexpected need for which no money was set aside. We should be saving as outlined in Action Step 5 (chap-

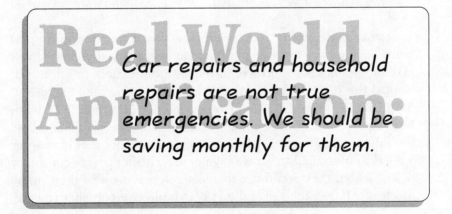

Car repairs and household repairs are not true emergencies. We should be saving monthly for them.

ter 7) for vacations, car repairs, Christmas, and other occasional expenses. However, we can't anticipate everything that might happen. For example, in a single year the roof may be damaged more than insurance will cover and a sewer line from your house to the street may need to be replaced, which could wipe out more than you saved.

Even when Elizabeth and I have saved money for emergencies and other expenses, I don't like having to spend it. I still struggle with a false sense of security about savings, and I don't like to pay for items that don't put us ahead financially. Having the money saved keeps us from falling behind when such expenses occur, but I have to stop and ask for God's forgiveness and then put things back into perspective almost every time it happens.

If the emergency involves replacement of something you need, consider buying a used item. It may take a little time and investigation to find a good buy, but the savings can be significant. One family I know suffered losses in a real estate venture in California more than ten years ago. The family chose not to declare bankruptcy and it has taken all these years to recover. Cruising through garage sales on Saturday mornings has become a favorite hobby. Family members also make it a matter of prayer if they need a shovel, a saucepan, a rug, or whatever. My faith is encouraged when I hear how God has met their needs because they ask him.

SAVING FOR EMERGENCIES WHILE PAYING DEBTS

Setting aside money for an emergency reserve (Action Step 8) while paying extra toward your home mortgage (Action Step 7) will take longer, because you will have less money each month to put toward this goal. An alternative would be putting Step 8 ahead of Step 7 and completely funding the emergency cash reserve first. I'm hesitant to recommend building your emergency reserve first because the time it takes might be discouraging. Remember that in chapter 9 the Robinsons had an extra $189 per month after paying consumer debts, which they could use to accelerate payment of their home mortgage? If they used all of the $189 to build an emergency reserve, they would have to put it in safe places such as money markets and savings accounts to make certain they didn't suffer investment losses. But these investments would only give them, as of this writing, about a 3 to 4 percent return. If they managed a 4 percent return, it would take over three years to accumulate $7,470 (two times the monthly income in the Robinsons' budget in fig. 4). This would require delaying an accelerated mortgage payoff much longer.

At Cornerstone, we usually don't recommend having a reserve fund strictly for emergencies until after the mortgage has been paid off. Middle-income families have so little money available to accomplish long-term goals and could easily become discouraged having to wait several years to fund them while they build an emergency reserve. Not having an emergency reserve is riskier, but savings for car replacement and cash reserves for vacations, car repairs, and gifts can double as an emergency reserve. Also, if a family chooses to accumulate funds to pay off a mortgage with one check, these funds can serve as an emergency reserve.

Rarely do people come to Cornerstone with four to five thousand dollars in savings. When they do, it's easy to prefund all the non-monthly spending categories and usually they even have a start on an emergency cash reserve.

Most people are like Karen and Richard Lively, who came in with the typical $19,000 in consumer debt and a $95,000 mortgage. Their income was under $50,000 and their passbook savings account held $971. We planned a balanced budget for all fourteen categories, and as always happens, there were unforeseen emergencies in the first twelve months. At first, the Livelys were trading money from one envelope to the next until the budget was finally refined.

It takes six months to a year to internalize the budgeting method and see it begin to work smoothly. But, through perseverance and our support, the Livelys kept focused on their ultimate goals. All the categories were funded and after several years, the emergency reserve was met. At the same time they made encouraging progress on paying off the consumer debt.

11

Please Send Money

THE PRICE of a college degree keeps going up—higher and faster than the rate of inflation. Babies born in 1993 will be ready to enter college in the year 2010, and by that time, it's estimated the cost of a four-year degree at the highest-rated private schools will be $60,000 or more a year.

The cost of state schools will be less, but still jolting. For today's middle incomers, scholarship funds have nearly dried up. Tightened budgets at higher educational institutions leave schools with less to give. Those of us with middle incomes may find we make too much to get help and too little to pay for college out of our pockets. Many of us are stuck with borrowing. Those low interest rates that took many baby boomers to college are gone now. If your child is an ethnic minority and you don't have many assets, you may be able to find need-based assistance, but even this may be less in coming years.

From talking with other parents, I know I'm not alone in dreaming of my son and daughter going to college. I also dream about how well they will do and what career they will choose. I put myself in their shoes, thinking about the good time I had leaving my hometown and living in my own apartment while attending a large state school. Looking back now, I had it made!

Most people I talk to don't realize what college costs will be until their children reach college age. The cost of college has increased dramatically over the last twenty years. Reality sets in when Dad does some

> **Real World Application:**
> *If it's impossible to pay off the mortgage before children start college, education saving should become the priority. Once college is completed, mortgage prepaying should be resumed.*

checking and is shocked to find he can't afford sending Junior to his alma mater. Also, if Junior is five feet, three inches tall and has a 2.9 grade point average, a basketball scholarship probably is not in the offing.

The least expensive option is for a young person to live at home and start out at a community college, earning an associate degree. Costs quickly escalate as you go from state universities to private colleges and Christian colleges, then to the Ivy League. The numbers below are taken from the 1997 Peterson's guide to two- and four-year colleges. These figures assume the student will live at home while attending a community college and that students attending state universities will attend one in their home state.

Broward Community College, Fort Lauderdale, Florida (public)
Tuition and Fees	$1,176

Arizona State University, Tempe, Arizona (public)
In-State Tuition and Fees	$1,950
Room and Board	$4,287
Total	$6,237

Wheaton College, Wheaton, Illinois (private)
Tuition and Fees	$12,300
Room and Board	$ 4,370
Total	$16,670

Harvard University, Cambridge, Massachusetts (private)

Tuition and Fees	$20,865
Room and Board	$ 6,710
Total	$27,575

Textbooks add from four hundred to seven hundred dollars per year, depending on the major. Transportation costs and incidentals are additional.

At Cornerstone, we find average parents contribute two thousand dollars each year to their child's education if the student lives at home. The average for kids going away to an in-state college is four thousand dollars from the parents each year.

College costs are mounting about 6 percent per year. With all the financial pressures, the typical middle-income family is finding it unrealistic to send children away to school and foot the bill. Plus, entrance requirements are much tougher and the only alternative left for many is the live-at-home, commute-to-junior-college option, at least to start. Here are a number of strategies.

COLLEGE SAVINGS STRATEGIES

Strategy 1

Save through investments.

Mark and Paula Robinson's children, Rhonda and Carl, are ages ten and seven. Rhonda will be old enough to start college in eight years, Carl in eleven. Let's assume the Robinsons plan to send both to a non-hometown state university for four years and this will be in today's dollars. Total cost for the degree should be around $28,000 ($7,000 x 4).

If the Robinsons' investments earn 10 percent, what amount (not counting inflation) must the family set aside each month to send Rhonda to school?

Rhonda's College Savings

Years to save:	8
Return on investment:	10%
Amount required:	$28,000
Amount set aside monthly:	$192

If the Robinsons could earn 10 percent (with more time, they might take more risk and look for a higher return), how much would they need to set aside each month for Carl's education?

Carl's College Savings

Years to save:	11
Return on investment:	10%
Amount required:	$28,000
Amount set aside monthly:	$117

Mark and Paula need to set aside $309 monthly to prefund their children's undergraduate education. We have ignored the annual increase in college costs to this point. For Rhonda, with an annual increase in costs of 6 percent, the Robinsons will pay a projected $45,000 in eight years. Carl's price tag could be $54,500 in eleven years. If they were funding these projected amounts rather than $28,000 for each child, the Robinsons would need to set aside $308 monthly for Rhonda and $226 for Carl, totaling $534.

Suppose they were able to save only $309 per month for the next eight years. Their children's college would be sorely underfunded. To allow for a projected 6 percent annual increase, a more realistic approach would be to increase their monthly contribution by twice the inflation rate, or 12 percent every year, rather than attempt to set aside almost twice that amount every month starting now. If they started with $309 this year, they would have to increase monthly savings to $346 ($309 x 1.12) next year, $388 the following year, and so on. Assuming Mark and Paula receive raises over the next ten years, an annual 12 percent increase in the monthly contribution should be achievable.

Strategy 2

Start saving for college when children are born.

If you haven't had children yet, the least painful way to fund a college education is to start saving for it when they are born. If the Robinsons had started when Rhonda was born, they would have had eighteen years to save instead of eight. Here are the numbers:

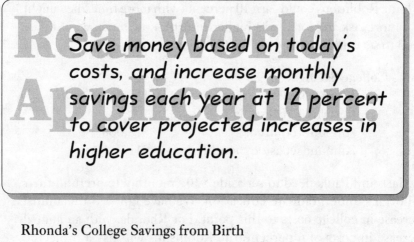

Save money based on today's costs, and increase monthly savings each year at 12 percent to cover projected increases in higher education.

Rhonda's College Savings from Birth

Years to save:	18
Return on investment:	10%
Amount needed:	$28,000
Set aside each month:	$47

The Robinsons' monthly funding would drop from $192 to $47. This shows the importance of identifying financial objectives and beginning to save for them as early as possible. They would need to increase the $47 monthly payment by 12 percent to keep up with rising college costs.

Strategy 3

Participate in a government prepaid college program.

Prefinancing a college education is growing in popularity. Not every state has it yet, but if your state does, this is an important strategy to consider. Florida is a trend setter in the area and, according to *The Florida Prepaid College Program* booklet, "The plan locks in and guarantees your child's college education at a fixed price." You don't have to be concerned about increasing costs if you utilize this plan. In Florida you can choose to prepay tuition alone or prepay tuition and dormitory bills. There are provisions for students who go to college out of state. Massachusetts and Florida have programs that can

be applied to state or private institutions. Some states have recipro-
cal arrangements, so look for this plan to become more flexible.

Rhonda is in the fourth grade, and to take advantage of the prepaid four-year tuition plan at a Florida university, the Robinsons
would pay $76 monthly (1995 numbers) until their daughter starts
college. A four-year dormitory contract is an additional $96 monthly,
for a total of $172. For Carl, who is in the first grade, the Robinsons
would pay $62 monthly. Carl's four-year dorm contract is an addi-
tional $75, totaling $137. The Robinsons would need $309.

The $309 is the same amount required in the previous strategy.
However, in the state program it is locked in and doesn't require
annual increases. It sounds so nice but I know you must have questions: "What if my child doesn't go to college or a vocational school?"
"What if my child gets a full scholarship?" In the Florida program,
you receive no interest, but you do get a full refund. Check into what
your state has to offer and consider that along with where you think
your child might attend. The only risk I see is that state prepaid college programs may discover several years down the road they can't
deliver what was promised at the previous price.

Strategy 4

Look into alternatives to prefunding college.

You may not have the time or resources to prefund college for one
or all of your children. There are other ways to go. Looking at the

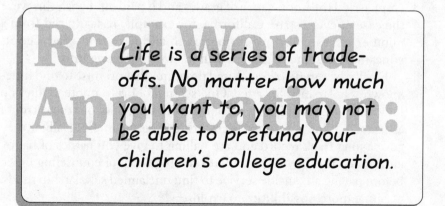

Real World Application:

Life is a series of trade-offs. No matter how much you want to, you may not be able to prefund your children's college education.

Robinsons' budget earlier in the book, we saw that they don't have the resources to set aside $309 now, unless they increase income or make significant cuts in spending. Life is a series of trade-offs. It takes a lot of prayer and sound thinking to make big decisions. You might want to investigate the following possibilities.

1. Funding college out of current cash flow.

If the mortgage and other debts are paid off, you could easily have several hundred dollars monthly and maybe more with which to help fund higher education.

2. Scholarships and grants.

It's important to start talking early to children about trying to do their best for the sake of scholarships. Not all college-bound kids are gifted academically, so we need to be careful. But if a child has academic or sports prowess, this becomes a possibility. Test scores on the SAT and ACT also play a role in obtaining some academic scholarships.

The former youth pastor of my home church was a lacrosse star. His ability in the sport paid his way through college. Guess what? Two of his boys showed promise, and he made playing the sport fun in their formative years. Both boys went on to good schools on almost full athletic scholarships.

One family had children with high grade-point averages. In Florida a high school GPA of 3.5 or higher qualifies a student for an automatic $2,500 annual scholarship. That translates to $10,000 of the four-year bill. One of the family's sons received another $6,000 over four years from the university. It's as if the state and university had written a check for $16,000 to the parents. As their children grew up, they emphasized the importance of grades and it paid off. I wish this were the case in every state. California, for example, has suffered from a number of years of slow or no growth and has greatly reduced its education assistance program. But it's worth looking into.

Finally, be careful of franchised programs that promise to find little-known scholarships for a fee. One selling tool is to quote studies on how many scholarships go unclaimed and then hold out the carrot of assistance. I don't want to discredit these services, especially if they have a long track record and are willing to give you names of happy customers. But I would start with the high school counseling office before paying an outside service to find unclaimed scholarship funds.

Some more possibilities to explore:

3. Co-op programs.

Try finding a college co-op program. Some institutions have built strong programs—such as in engineering—around the concept of going to school, then spending time on the job. Some companies use this as a recruiting tool. The student starts working while earning a degree, then works full-time after graduation.

4. Working through school.

Working while going to school is popular, especially where students don't live on campus. At Nova Southeastern University where I teach, most of our students work full or part time. Holding a full-time job and attending college isn't easy, but students choosing this route believe it's worth it. Sometimes it's the only way.

5. Borrowing.

I'm one of those parents who always said I would never borrow to finance my children's education. But Cornerstone founder Jim Underwood reminds me this is not always realistic. Borrowing several thousand dollars each year may not be a great idea, but there may be a legitimate need to bridge a small gap with some borrowing. One of my former university students told me that he and his wife had borrowed one hundred thousand dollars for their higher education. Jim Underwood and I suggest you treat borrowing for college as a last resort. I have many clients who have lived to regret going to college by borrowing, as they try to pay off loans while raising a family.

6. Military service.

Since the introduction of the GI Bill at the end of World War II, thousands have benefited from college educations they otherwise could not have afforded. While changes have been made, an armed forces recruiter will be more than willing to walk you through the educational benefits from Uncle Sam. If your child's grades and test scores are high, you may want to consider applying for an appointment to one of the military academies. Tuition, room, and board are free and cadets are paid small salaries. After four years, a graduate holds a degree from a prestigious school and is a commissioned officer. Normally a multiyear commitment to military service is required in return.

7. Grandparents' contribution.

Grandparents often figure into funding college educations. You may not have much say in this process, but if you do, you can work together. I know one family in which grandparents are putting $100 a month into a savings account. The parents are able to save $50. Our recommendation was to pool the $150 into a mutual fund earning 10 percent or more. In some mutual funds that operate under the Uniform Gifts Act the money given is owned by the child and is not accessible until the child reaches eighteen. There are no taxes to pay until the money is removed. The downside is that you have no control over how your child uses the money.

8. Delaying college to save.

You can always delay starting college while saving the money. If Christians believe that God wants them to go to college and they can't find the money, God will provide the way, but it may take a little more time. If you or your child are in this situation, it may be tough to have someone say this to you when you have waited for what has seemed like forever. Keep praying and ask others to join you in prayer. God may use someone you least expect to open the right door.

9. Qualifying for college financial assistance.

Frequently, I get questions about reducing debt and the impact it might have on obtaining financial assistance to pay for children's college education. It almost seems that we should keep ourselves in bad shape financially to qualify for college financial aid, but that isn't true. If you have substantial liquid assets (money markets, CDs, stocks, bonds, and mutual funds) and debt, the best thing to do is use the assets to pay off all debts—including the mortgage if possible. The presence of liquid assets can reduce eligibility for financial assistance, but equity in a personal residence and assets in retirement funds have no effect.

HELPING YOUR CHILDREN CHOOSE A CAREER

I am convinced that God has a calling for each believer. It just takes some of us longer than others to discover our calling. All phases of our lives come under his grace, including ways in which we minister and where we should work. Seeking his will and leadership also should apply to future occupations.

A mistake many make when heading off to college is not taking steps to determine what career path God wants for them and what education they need. All of us know people who wanted to be a doctor or lawyer since childhood. They go to college, go to graduate school, become successful, and live happily ever after. They are exceptions. Many of us don't know what we want to do with our lives, so we change majors in college and end up working in jobs unrelated to our degrees.

I'm a good example. I was an architecture major as a freshman. Then I decided to go to law school and changed my major to history. In preparation for law school, it was recommended that I take a course in accounting principles. There I discovered my area of strength. One course followed another until I ended up with a minor in accounting. Instead of law school, I obtained a master's degree in accounting and went on to become a CPA.

I still wasn't fulfilled. As I've told you, it wasn't until I later started teaching, consulting, and advising families on personal finances that I was truly fulfilled in my career. Because I enjoy my work immensely and have the opportunity to minister through my work, I believe I am where God has called me to be.

Going through all this searching for purpose cost me dearly financially and resulted in many disappointments. Others who graduated with me were advancing in their careers while I was going from one job to another trying to find "my thing." Now that I have discovered a career path that seems to utilize my God-given gifts, talents, and motivational patterns, work has gone from being a source of dread to a source of joy. Now I see that God used my frustrations and mistakes to prepare me for my calling.

I discover in counseling that others are like me in not wanting their children to make the same mistakes. We can't make the decision of how many trials God wants our children to endure before they finally "settle down," but we can help them discover their strengths and weaknesses and see how these could relate to a future vocation. We have discovered two services that provide similar aid:

1. Larry Burkett's organization, Christian Financial Concepts, has a related ministry called Career Pathways. For a little over $100, Career Pathways offers a lengthy questionnaire assessing a person's God-given personality, interests, and abilities, and results in an in-depth analysis of what careers might be the most fulfilling.

2. Maximum Potential helps people discover their gifts through an approach slightly different from that of Career Pathways.

I suggest you contact both (see appendix E) and decide which is best in helping your child assess the future.

We believe parents should help their children receive as much education as they need. But just as important is to help them make wise decisions. That's why we suggest you use one of these two services. Be forewarned, a totalitarian attitude on your part is apt to provoke your child to rebellion. Spiritual growth is at work in both parents and children. Treat their future as a spiritual adventure in which children and parents share. Pray together and remember that parents of older teenagers need to be listeners more than talkers to keep relationships open.

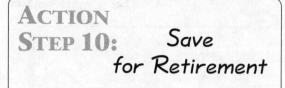

12

A Nest Egg
for Your Golden Years

IT'S NEVER TOO LATE. What an encouragement for baby boomers who haven't yet saved peanuts for retirement. In 1996 baby boomers began turning fifty and already people by the millions in the generation ahead of them are having to work an extra ten years to make ends meet. With the future of Social Security in doubt and pension plans canceled right and left, individuals can't count on an employer or the U.S. Treasury to provide for retirement.

The *Denver Post* in 1995 referred to a survey by Colonial Life and Accident Insurance that showed "the amount workers saved for retirement dropped 8 percent in 1994 and is off 34 percent in the last two years. Another survey, by Godwins, Booke and Dickenson, a benefits education specialist, found that a third of all boomers have less than $10,000 saved."

Kind of scary, isn't it? It is, especially if this applies to you. And quoting even more findings, the *Post* reported "four in ten set aside less than $1,000 last year." A *USA Today*/CNN/Gallup Poll showed "at the same time, two-thirds expect to live as well—or better—in retirement as they do today." We expect to live better, but we forget that we will also live longer.

Why then, might you ask, is saving for retirement the *final* action step?

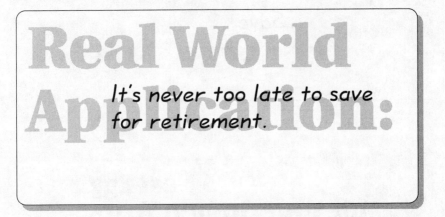

It's never too late to save for retirement.

First, if we still have consumer debt and car notes at high interest rates, it doesn't make sense to invest retirement funds earning 10 to 12 percent, while paying 14 percent or higher on our debt. Second, it doesn't make sense to borrow for our children's college while investing heavily in a retirement program. Third, having a house paid for is a sound financial base for the retirement years.

Even if you turn fifty before starting to save for retirement, you can build a sizable sum because there should be so much more to invest each month if you accomplished the previous steps.

Look again at the Robinsons. At Mark and Paula's current income level, if their children finish college, and the mortgage and other debts are paid off, they will have $1,386 to apply monthly to a retirement fund. The $697 mortgage payment, $189 debt payments, and $500 private school tuition add up to a sizable amount to tuck away.

Ignoring what they've already managed to hold onto, by saving $1,386 per month starting at age fifty and earning 10 percent, they should have $574,000 by age sixty-five. Add to that the $17,300 already saved for retirement (see fig. 1), which would have grown to $77,000 by age fifty, and the total saved grows to $917,000 by sixty-five. With no mortgage payments, the Robinsons can live better on part of the interest than they did while working, even after factoring in inflation.

Of course, it works much more easily if you start putting money away early in your working life. One of my clients had a high-paying position in his twenties and did not get married until he was thirty. He laments, "If only I had started saving for retirement in my twenties. Not only would saving habits have been established, but I would have another twenty years of compounding." By waiting until his forties to start funding a KEOGH retirement plan, he must really stretch each year to keep putting in money. With three children, including two teenagers, he can't make retirement payments the highest priority.

At Cornerstone, we are thrilled when a twenty-year-old comes in and starts socking money away for the postworking years. Habits set in our twenties have a better chance of sticking, even with marriage and the arrival of children.

A twenty-two-year-old who works forty-five years and makes a salary of $3,000 monthly who can save 10 percent of income for retirement for that length of time will end up with $3,144,750 by maintaining a return on investment of 10 percent.

Starting that early provides a number of options, such as beginning a second career before retirement or retiring earlier than normal to pursue a nonpaying position with a church or mission agency.

Marjorie and Bill Johnson are in their twenties with a one-year-old to raise. Bill makes $38,000 each year with no retirement program. Marjorie works part time and leaves their daughter with Bill's mother for twenty hours a week. The Johnsons have established IRAs, contributing $334 per month ($167 each). In thirty years, at an interest rate of 10 percent, the Johnsons will have built up a retirement nest egg of $752,740.

WHY YOU SHOULD SAVE FOR RETIREMENT

Why should we save for retirement? I've been told this shows a lack of dependence upon the Lord to provide for our needs. I strongly disagree. As Christians, we should certainly keep a check on our motives as we save for retirement. The Bible supports saving to meet future needs, but we must ask ourselves at the same time if our dependency is on God or on our accumulated savings. Ron Blue asked in his book *Master Your Money*, "Is it wrong, then, to have a long-term goal of financial independence? I believe not—unless financial independence is defined as having enough to be independent of God."

The Bible, of course, tells us that "the wise man saves for the future, but the foolish man spends whatever he gets" (Prov. 21:20 LB). God's Word never uses the word retirement in the sense we use the word. Our work for the Lord is never done. The oldest saints in Scripture continued their life's work until the Lord called them home. Yes, times are different and the steel plant may not want you around. However, Christians must review their calling and ask what God wants them to do once they cease to earn a paycheck. Nowhere in Scripture is there a concept of taking life easy. Instead, there seems to be the idea of working as we're able until we enter the final rest.

Accumulating enough to retire is the same as becoming financially independent. Some of our clients have achieved this and that's what Elizabeth and I are working toward, but not so we can retire. If God continues to provide us with the resources to achieve financial independence, I believe it will be because he wants us to do something productive for him without concern for making a living. Even if I continued working part time, we would be in a position to give away more than ever before. The key is to find work in our retirement years that glorifies God.

Don't misunderstand me, however. If you have the resources, I'm not saying never take the vacation of your dreams and I'm not saying never eat out. I believe God wants us to enjoy his creation and see as much as we can. But I don't think he wants us to end up like many of the retirees I see in South Florida who become literally bored to death.

Instead, I think of one couple we know who volunteer nine months out of the year in our church and then head north during the summer to visit their children and help out in work projects for a missions agency. They are in their seventies, but their health is good and they lead full and rewarding lives. By traveling to new work projects each summer, they have time to explore new parts of the country. Because they saved ahead, they work for free.

Another reason you should save for retirement is the uncertain future of Social Security. Many people don't know that if they were born after 1938, retirement age starts increasing until those born after 1959 can't start receiving full Social Security benefits until age sixty-seven. This is thanks to the Tax Reform Act of 1986. Based on projected shortfalls in needed taxes to meet projected benefit payouts, further changes in eligibility for benefits should be expected.

If the Robinsons factor in Social Security based on current expectations, they will need less for retirement savings. They are both thirty-five and with a current annual income of $54,000 can hope for Social Security benefits of about $20,000 annually. Their savings would only have to provide $34,000 a year.

In our personal planning—and I recommend this for you, too—Elizabeth and I do not factor Social Security into our savings. Save for retirement as if there were no Social Security. The amount of the benefits and when they will be paid is unpredictable beyond the next fifteen to twenty years. If you do receive anything from Uncle Sam, enjoy the bonus.

To find out what you might get from Social Security, stop by your local office or call 800-234-5772. Ask for form SSA–7004 called "Request for Earnings and Benefit Estimate Statement." This will help you come close to knowing what the government at this time expects to send you after age sixty-five or in more cases, age sixty-seven.

Real World Application:

Save for retirement as if there were no Social Security.

How Much You Should Save

Experience shows that when people retire, their monthly household expenses drop. Charles Schwab and Company's booklet *Guide to Retirement Planning* says to expect retirement spending to take about 70 percent of your current income. It also points out that expenses in some areas may go up, including health, travel, recreation, and entertainment. We suggest clients use current income as a guide to estimate income needs at retirement, using today's dollars. If they need less income upon retiring, they have more options. Considering the number of years people live past retirement, it is wise to plan for more than you think you will need when you stop earning a paycheck.

If you are unable to save enough to provide a retirement income equal to what you make while working, you must plan to either lower your style of living or work part time as a retiree. To avoid that problem, be willing to cut back on your lifestyle while still working.

To project what clients need for retirement income, we recommend they have a goal of saving ten times their current income. Using this rule of thumb, the Robinsons would need to accumulate $540,000 (10 x $54,000) by retirement in today's dollars, ignoring any Social Security benefits.

Everyone has different circumstances, and that makes it more important to receive qualified advice. To decide where and how to place your retirement dollars, we recommend you proceed with care. You can start with fee-only financial planners. Many CPAs are quite knowledgeable and willing to help. Find an expert who isn't getting a commission for selling an investment product to help you set goals. You can, of course, also contact Cornerstone. As to where to put your money, we've included resources to consider in appendix E.

Inflation will reduce the buying power of the Robinsons' $54,000 annual income over the next fifteen years, the time they have to save for retirement if they start at age fifty and retire at age sixty-five. To keep up with inflation and maintain their standard of living, they need to have saved much more than $540,000. With a 4 percent annual inflation rate, they would need to have $983,000 by age sixty-five to have the equivalent earning power of $540,000 today. That

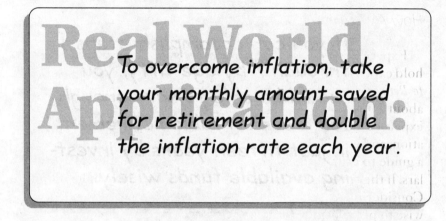

To overcome inflation, take your monthly amount saved for retirement and double the inflation rate each year.

would require setting aside $1,544 every month to reach their goal of $983,000 by sixty-five, if they can earn 10 percent and their current retirement funds continue to grow.

Because of their current retirement funds balance of $17,300 (see fig. 1), which would grow to $77,000 by age fifty at a 10 percent earning rate without the addition of one more dime, the Robinsons aren't in bad shape in terms of retirement. When we sit down with many of our clients and work out a retirement game plan, many are surprised to discover it is quite achievable, even though they feel buried in debt. The key is doing something now to chart a new course financially, or the retirement goals may not be achievable.

But suppose the Robinsons did not have a retirement funds balance that could grow to $77,000 by age fifty. To reach their goal of accumulating $983,000 by age sixty-five, they would need to set aside $2,370 every month if they were earning 10 percent. This would be impossible.

We recommend that our clients handle inflation by increasing their monthly savings for retirement each year by double the inflation rate. Assuming an inflation rate of 4 percent, the Robinsons could start by saving monthly the $1,386 we pointed out earlier they had available, and increase it by 8 percent one year later. That would make it $1,497 monthly ($1,386 x 1.08) in the second year, $1,617 monthly ($1,497 x 1.08) in the third year, and so on. With an annual raise from their jobs and all other financial goals achieved, the required annual saving increases should be more than feasible. With proper planning,

> *If you can accomplish Steps 1 through 9 by age fifty, you should be able to save enough for a comfortable retirement in just fifteen years by investing available funds wisely.*

the Robinsons could accumulate enough on a moderate income for retirement in just fifteen years, even if they had no funds at age fifty.

If you can accomplish Steps 1 through 9 by age fifty, you should be able to save enough for a comfortable retirement in just fifteen years by investing available funds wisely. If by age forty you are not well on your way to completion of Action Steps 1 through 9, begin setting aside something for retirement, even as little as fifty dollars a month. If your employer offers a retirement plan that matches your savings, take advantage of this to leverage more money for the future.

Thirteen Tips for Making the Right Retirement Choices

1. *Set aside pretax dollars.*

   Pretax dollars grow faster. Take advantage of your company 401(k), 403(b), KEOGH, or SEP. You can start taking money out at age fifty-nine and a half without penalty.

2. *Invest in IRAs.*

   IRAs are still a good way to save because of their tax-deferred feature, especially if you are closing in on retirement and are already contributing the maximum allowed by law at work.

3. *Don't write the check.*

   Find a way to have retirement money withdrawn from your paycheck automatically and monthly. Dollar cost averaging (a set amount invested regularly over the long term) works.

4. *Don't go for high-fliers to make up for lost time.*

Sure, if you had put $450 five years ago in Herbalife and Nature's Bounty, you would now have $48,000. But dart-board investing and market timing are incorrect strategies for retirement savings. Look to place your money in investments (probably mutual funds) with long track records of 10 percent or more. Don't buy mutual funds just because they are at the top of the charts this year. They rise high but they can fall hard.

5. *Diversify.*

The resources at the end of the book contain information about spreading your risk, especially as you have more to invest. Stocks traditionally have provided the best growth. Reinvesting gains and dividends complement the increasing war chest.

6. *Buy no-load or no-commission mutual funds.*

Although there is now some evidence that it evens out after several years, buy no-load or no-commission mutual funds. The theory is if you start out with more in, there will be more to take out later.

7. *Plan with the Rule of 72.*

This helps you know how long it takes an investment to double. Divide 72 by the rate of return. If you are getting as much as 14 percent on a mutual fund, your investment will double in 5.2 years (72 divided by 14). It takes 7.2 years to double an investment earning 10 percent.

8. *Buy a smaller house.*

If you are fifty-five or older, sell your paid-for house and move into something smaller. You have a capital gains deduction on up to $125,000 in profits earned from selling that house. This is a one-time benefit. You could also consider moving to a cheaper part of the country.

9. *Have a will prepared.*

Many computer programs can help you write your will, but you want guidance from a highly trained professional who sees all your assets and hears your goals and carries them out within your local state law. Seven of ten people still have no will. If you don't have one drawn by the time you die, the state has one ready. It probably wouldn't dispose of your assets as you would like.

10. *Investigate a living trust, especially if your estate will contain mainly securities or out-of-state property.*

    This can get complicated, and the myth is that you save on estate taxes. You do gain the benefit of bypassing probate costs and a public inspection of your estate.

11. *Consider a life insurance trust.*

    If you have a big policy and your retirement package is over $1.2 million for a couple, your heirs will get a big surprise when you die and the life insurance proceeds result in taxes due. The answer is to put part or all of the ownership in the names of your children or other loved ones. Or you can fund a life insurance trust that can provide an income for the surviving spouse and pass on to children when the spouse dies.

12. *Establish a family trust if your estate will move above $1.2 million.*

    There's a more complicated name for this: credit shelter trust. It can double the amount of assets a married couple may pass on to heirs.

13. *Establish a charitable trust.*

    Charitable trusts come in various shapes and sizes but can help reduce taxes, provide income now, and upon your death, help support causes about which you care.

Getting Started

CONSIDER Jerry Goodrick, people person, most-likely-to-succeed and natural salesman living as if life is a party. Turning his love for people into a satisfying career selling insurance and investments, Jerry is generous to everyone around him. People enjoy buying from him because he truly cares. Singlehood for Jerry means always picking up the tab at lunch. Marriage means meeting every desire of his new wife. He loves giving presents. But money runs out quickly on a $50,000 salary with a $100,000 lifestyle.

Now see Jerry standing at the door of Cornerstone with his shoulders hunched forward, his head lowered. Above his medium-build frame is a face drawn by exhaustion, tanned in the Florida sun but looking much older than his forty-two years. Jerry is clean, but he has a forgot-to-shave beard and dirt under his fingernails. Debt has overcome him. His job is a six-dollars-an-hour landscaping position, offered by a friend with a free bedroom. His wife has taken the two boys and left him. The house is repossessed. Creditors have seized everything. Deeply depressed, he is here at the recommendation of a friend.

On the day Jerry came to us, my colleague, Jim Underwood, tried conducting a financial inventory but was unsuccessful. Jerry was beyond bankruptcy. His entire identity had collapsed. All his hopes of having the perfect job, the perfect marriage, and the perfect children were gone. With them were Jerry's self-concept and reason for living.

Jerry was so far down that his Cornerstone meetings never went beyond emotional counseling, drenched in prayer. At his last meeting, in between convulsive sobs, he said, "Jim, all I ever wanted to do was be a man of God." Nothing Jim said could penetrate the wall of grief and offer a ray of hope.

One week after that last meeting, Jerry came down the stairs from his bedroom looking as if he finally had a purpose again. Telling his friend, and employer-landlord, "Something has to change! I can't take this anymore!" Jerry ran out the door. He drove his well-used Chevy to a cornfield outside Zellwood, got out, ran an old hose from the tailpipe into the back window, restarted the car and leaned back, never to awaken in this world again.

Jerry had decided a $250,000 life insurance policy was worth more to his family than his life. He thought he could give them one last present.

Jim Underwood can hardly tell this story without breaking down, and it is difficult for me to relate it to you. I have because it dramatically illustrates the deep power money can hold over our lives. When we buy into the world's perspective that money is the measure of the man, our entire identity is wrapped up in our earning power and the value of our possessions. We can end up, as Jerry did, in powerless despair.

GOD'S UNFAILING LOVE

This chapter is titled "Getting Started," and looking at it from the outside, getting started should be simple. It's just a matter of beginning at Step 1 and following the simple suggestions that will lead to your goal. But it's not always that easy. I said before that the real Step 1 is prayer. We need to do more than pray for God's help to change. We need to ask him to expose this false identity that comes from the world and get a firm grasp on his grace. Otherwise we can be so swamped by a sense of failure that, like Jerry, we will never be able to take the first step, much less reach our goals. We need to understand God's perspective of our priceless value apart from anything we have or earn. Then we can move ahead with freedom and hope.

Countless verses in the Bible tell us the extent of God's unconditional love, but the story of the prodigal son goes right to the heart of the matter. (See Luke 15:11–31.) The son had recklessly spent his inheritance with a callous disregard for virtue or his father's feelings. Yet the message that comes through from the beginning is the father's deep love for his son regardless of what he had done.

Jesus tells the story to illustrate that it is not just the obedient, faithful son the father loves. His love for the disreputable failure of a son is such that simply having that son home again is the only issue. There is no recrimination, no cool withholding of affection. On the contrary, the father simply rejoices, "This is my son." And that says it all.

This is our identity as believers. "You are all sons of God through faith in Christ Jesus" (Gal. 3:26). We have the same abiding personal love from our heavenly Father that the prodigal received from his father. We must believe this in the face of everything the world says to the contrary. Jerry's only really important failure was his refusal to believe that his heavenly Father valued him regardless of his past.

The Father's love surrounds us now and always will. He will always forgive us and receive us back after we mess up, not with exasperation, but with the robe and the ring and the fatted calf. Beyond that acceptance we have an inheritance from him that will never fade, kept in heaven, and a promise of his fatherly care and provision in

Truth: *God's love for us as his children is the foundation we need to begin to change.*

this life. We can face the fact that our financial life hasn't been so much a matter of failure but of sin when we realize that he willingly forgives us and promises to help us with every step down the road of obedience. God's love for us as his children is the foundation we need to begin to change.

TAKE THE FIRST STEP

Moving from knowing what we should do to doing it takes faith. Sheer determination may carry us a little way down the road, but when habitual behaviors reassert themselves and discouragement hits us in the face, determination will vanish like a mist. We need faith to obey, or what the Bible calls "the obedience that comes from faith" (Rom. 1:5).

If you have failed repeatedly, perhaps tried other methods and given up after a while, and if you are facing overwhelming debt, then the commandments of God concerning finances will feel like a pile of bricks on your back. But the Lord Jesus says he doesn't load you up with heavy requirements. He promises to give you rest from heavy burdens of responsibility and to replace them with a yoke that is light. The apostle John tells us the requirements of God are not burdensome (1 John 5:3).

I believe this is because God's commandments contain a promise. While they keep us from drifting comfortably along a disobedient path, they also assure us of what God will do in our lives if we trust

Truth:

The obedience of faith means taking the first step, trusting God to accomplish the results.

him. The obedience of faith simply means taking that first step in confidence that the Lord is yoked together with you bearing the load. He will take you where he wants you to go. The Holy Spirit will bring about the deep inner change you need to begin living differently. And as the Word of God says, "He who began a good work in you will carry it on to completion" (Phil. 1:6).

The obedience of faith means taking the first step, trusting God to accomplish the results. The obedience of faith also involves perseverance or, to put it another way, being able to pick up and start again, again and again.

God's Word convicted me that the way I was handling our money was far from pleasing to him. Whenever I falter along the road to change, this conviction keeps me from feeling comfortable with my old habits. But only faith in the love and grace of God enables me to recommit to the task. Without this faith, Jerry's solution sometimes seems like the only way out of our predicament.

Once new habits start to form, it's not so hard. You see results and become encouraged. But at first, it takes sheer faith in God to pick yourself up and start again.

From my experience, two barriers get in the way.

The first is a sense of failure. You feel guilty. You think, "This is the real me; I can't ever change." Don't believe it. Who you are in Christ is someone quite different from who you are when you rely on your own strengths and abilities. If the Lord requires a change, he will not leave you to your own devices. The Spirit is at work in you. He will bring about the change.

The second barrier is perfectionism. If you are like me, you don't want to do something unless you can do it right. So when you get behind, you try to catch up on all the undone paperwork. Forget it. Let it go. Just start again and keep going.

Sometimes we do everything right and still see little change in our financial circumstances. At these discouraging lows, I always seem to hear someone's testimony about how God miraculously helped them pay off $40,000 in credit-card bills in eighteen months with an annual family income of $35,000. Ugh!

Be at peace that you are attempting to be obedient. Leave the results to the Lord to accomplish in his time.

TRUST GOD

How can we trust God to change us at those times when we are in the grip of our own agenda—at those times when we don't want to change? Psalm 37:4 says, "Delight yourself in the LORD and he will give you the desires of your heart." This is an amazing promise and I have seen it fulfilled in my life many times.

When I was six years old my family took a vacation trip through the whole state of Florida. I loved Florida and I decided then that I was going to move to Fort Lauderdale some day.

Twenty-five years later I had given up on that desire and a lot of intervening desires and was finally at the point of joyfully surrendering to God's agenda for my life. We were trying to get our finances in order as a matter of obedience to the Lord and I was looking for a job. An old friend invited us to visit him in Fort Lauderdale and, remembering how much I loved it as a child, I was delighted to accept. We had been saving for vacation and paying off the debt we had accumulated on credit cards. Then I finished our tax return and discovered that we owed several hundred dollars. Paying the IRS took every last cent of the money we had saved for months to take the trip. I called my friend and told him what had happened and declined his invitation. He encouraged us to come anyway, but I was unwilling to do it on credit or without any money saved.

It didn't seem fair. I had tried to do what was right with our finances for a change, and this was the result. I struggled in prayer with my sense of injustice and came away realizing that I mistakenly thought God owed me a smooth road in return for my attempts at obedience. I repented of my presumption and simply asked the Lord to provide the funds if he wanted us to make the trip.

Within two days the needed money became available from an unexpected source. I called my friend and told him we would be there after all.

I hadn't been to Fort Lauderdale since I was six, and when we arrived it all came back to me—the sun and the sea breeze and the blue, blue sky, the palm trees, and best of all, the rolling turquoise ocean meeting pure, white sandy beaches. To my surprise, the whole family shared my enthusiasm.

After Elizabeth and I prayed about it, I began pursuing job possibilities in Fort Lauderdale. Months of fruitless searching in the town where we lived hadn't prepared me for the response I got in Fort Lauderdale. A few weeks after our vacation I was headed back for several interviews. Not only did I receive a job offer, but I found a job for Elizabeth.

The Lord does give us our desires when we delight ourselves in him. Of course, there are no guarantees that things will always turn out this way. Many times when I turn over my desires to the Lord, he doesn't give them to me, but when I have asked him to take a desire away if it doesn't conform to his will, he mysteriously does just that. I wake up one day and the desire is gone.

Two more practical suggestions for practicing the obedience of faith:

1. *Soak yourself in the Word of God.*

   At Cornerstone we incorporate Scripture into our counseling because we know it has the power to bring about deep conviction and change. There is no better way to break the power of the world's point of view and begin to see things from God's perspective than to read the Bible, memorize the verses we need most, and meditate in dependence on the Holy Spirit on what God is saying to us. (See appendix D for a number of good verses as a beginning.)

2. *Seek godly counsel.*

   Our American culture has taught us to be independent thinkers and to stand on our own two feet. But God's Word tells us the wise man will "listen to advice and accept instruction" (Prov. 19:20). Where can we hear good advice? First, from the Bible, but secondly and crucially, we need to heed the words of godly people. Whenever you have a decision to make or find yourself in a dilemma, pray, study the Word, and seek the counsel of believers whose lives reflect holiness and self-control. And discuss things with your spouse. Elizabeth has been a valuable source of wisdom about our finances and my business activities.

Other believers also can encourage you and hold you accountable as you walk down the road to financial freedom. This is Cornerstone's calling and expertise. I invite you to call us. We have trained CPAs who can work with you for as long as it takes.

More Help from Cornerstone

Afterword

IN 1985 Cornerstone Management Associates, Inc. was founded in Orlando, Florida. Jim Dean joined Cornerstone in 1990 and is now director of associate development.

After many years of teaching Christians the essentials of money management from a biblical perspective in seminars nationwide, Cornerstone founder Jim Underwood saw a problem with implementation of those principles. Seminars failed to produce lasting changes and workbooks usually ended up gathering dust. As a result, Jim established Cornerstone, a one-to-one discipling ministry that results in remarkable turnarounds in people's financial circumstances.

In 1996 Jim Underwood and a group of Cornerstone associates founded The Institute for Debt Free Living. The purpose of the Institute is found in its mission statement: "The Institute is an established business for the purpose of ministry through helping people implement biblical financial principles." The Institute's major emphasis is on the principle of becoming debt-free and experiencing the joy that position can bring.

There are other organizations dedicated to helping people become debt-free, but what sets the Institute apart is the Tele-coaching program. Through a series of personal one-to-one sessions based on the highly successful Cornerstone model, a trained personal advisor customizes a step-by-step plan by telephone or in person that is both simple and attainable. The personal advisor will establish a series of one-to-one sessions as follows:

- Three weekly meetings to design and implement a balanced budget in the home
- Three monthly meetings to establish a plan to achieve long term goals
- Quarterly sessions thereafter for the purpose of monitoring progress

Once assigned, the personal advisor will continue with the client to help update personalized plans and keep the client accountable.

The Institute also makes available a marketing program providing a part-time income to apply toward becoming debt free.

If you would like a free copy of our *Smart Spending Guide* or information about the Institute and its programs, please contact us:

The Institute for Debt Free Living
930 Woodcock Road, Suite 105
Orlando, FL 32803
Phone: (407) 895-5200
Fax: (407) 895-3525

Appendix A

Examples
and Blank Forms

Figure 1
The Robinsons' Personal Financial Statement

Date: _August 31_

Assets (present market value)

1. Cash/assets easily converted to cash
   a. Cash on hand and checking account $ 692
   b. Savings   –0–
   c. Money market funds   –0–
   d. Marketable stocks and bonds
   e. Cash value of life insurance
   f. Coins
2. Real estate
   a. Home   105,000
   b. Other real estate
3. Receivables
   a. Mortgage receivables
   b. Notes receivables
4. Business valuation
5. Personal property
   a. Automobiles   15,000 ← Ford Taurus $11,000
   b. Furniture   5,000   Honda Accord $ 4,000
   c. Jewelry   2,000
   d. Boat
   e. Other   camper   4,500
6. Retirement
   a. IRA   4,800
   b. Pension/retirement plan   12,500
7. Miscellaneous

Total Assets $ 149,492

Liabilities (current amount owed)

1. Current bills $ 800
2. Real estate
   a. Home mortgage   95,000
   b. Other mortgages
3. Personal debts to relatives
4. Business loans
5. Educational loans   4,000
6. Automobile loans   7,800
7. Credit cards   4,400
8. Medical bills
9. Life insurance loans
10. Bank loans
11. Installment loans   225
12. Credit union loans

Total Liabilities $ 112,225
Total Assets - Total Liabilities = Net Worth $ 37,267

Figure 2
The Robinsons' List of Debts

Date: ___Avgvst 31___

Creditor	For What	Monthly Payment	Remaining Payments	Balance Due	Interest Rate	Scheduled Payoff Date
Visa		$ 60	?	$2,800	16.0%	
FMC	Ford	263	34 mos.	7,800	10.0%	
FNB	edvc	89	51 mos.	4,000	6.0%	
Discover		40	?	1,600	16.9%	
Firestone	tires	30	8 mos.	225	19.0%	
Total		$482		$16,425	12.0% avg rate	
$16,425 balance @ $482 monthly payment @12% interest = 42 months left						
Add $70 per month = $552 monthly payment						
$16,425 balance @ $552 monthly payment @12% interest = 36 mos. left						
Mortgage						
Sun Trust						
Bank	home	$697	26 years	$95,000	8.0%	
Totals						

Figure 3
The Robinsons' Estimated Monthly Budget Unbalanced

Date: _August 31_

1. Income			**Monthly Amount**	
Wages, husband:	gross_____	net*	$	2,700
Wages, wife:	gross_____	net*	$	595
Dividends				
Interest earned				
Net rents				
Net business income				
Pension/retirement				
Other				
Total Income:			$	3,295

*Net wages are gross wages minus federal, state, and local income
tax, Social Security, and other benefits withheld from paycheck.

2. Giving			
Church	410		
Other	20		
Total Giving:		$	430

3. Savings			
Short term savings			
Long term savings			
Retirement savings Paula's IRA	50		
Other savings ($100 w/h from Mark's paycheck)			
Total Savings:		$	50

4. Housing			
Rent or mortgage	800		
Property taxes } In mortgage			
Property insurance payment			
Electricity	110		
Heating/gas			
Water	40		
Garbage service			
Cable TV	20		
Telephone	55		
Cleaning			
Repairs/maintenance	-0-		
Supplies			
Improvements	50		
Furnishings			
Other			
Total Housing:		$	1,075

Figure 3
The Robinsons' Estimated Monthly Budget Unbalanced
(continued)

5. Food

Groceries		$	375
Eating out			
School lunches			25
Other			
Total Food:		$	400

6. Clothing/Grooming

Purchases	70
Cleaning	15
Hair care	30
Toiletries/cosmetics	15
Total Clothing:	$ 130

7. Transportation (car payment in Debt Repayment)

Gas and oil	70
Automobile insurance	120
Repair and maintenance	30
Licenses/registration	
Parking and tolls	
Public transportation	
Other	
Total Transportation:	$ 220

8. Medical

Doctor	10
Dentist	10
Prescriptions	10
Glasses	
Health insurance ($120 per mo. w/h	
Other from paycheck)	
Total Medical:	$ 30

9. Children

School tuition	500
Allowances	16
School lunch	
Tutoring	
Music/dance lessons	10
Tennis/sports	10
Babysitting	15
Other	
Total Children:	$ 551

Figure 3
The Robinsons' Estimated Monthly Budget Unbalanced
(continued)

10. Debt Repayment

    Total from Debt List (consumer debt only): $ 482

11. Insurance

    Life insurance *($480 paid annually)* $ 40

    Disability

    Other

    Total Insurance: $ 40

12. Recreation

    Adult allowances   120

    Vacations   100

    Magazines/newspapers   10

    Books/tapes/records

    Subscriptions

    Hobbies

    Entertainment   100

    Pets (vet, license)

    Other

    Total Recreation: $ 330

13. Gifts

    Christmas   50

    Birthdays   20

    Anniversaries

    Weddings/showers

    Graduations

    Office gifts   10

    Other

    Total Gifts: $ 80

14. Other Personal/Business

    Clubs, union dues

    Accounting/legal *taxes*   10

    Cornerstone

    Other   *miscellaneous*   50

    Total Other Personal/Business: $ 60

    Total Spending: $ 3,878

    Net Margin/Deficit: $ <583>

Figure 4
The Robinsons' Estimated Monthly Budget Balanced

Date: _August 31_

1. Income

			Monthly Amount	
Wages, husband:	gross _____	net*	$ _____ 2,700	+100
Wages, wife:	gross _____	net*	$ _____ 595	
Dividends			_____	
Interest earned			_____	
Net rents			_____	
Net business income			_____	
Pension/retirement			_____	
Other	teaching		_____	+340
Total Income:			$ _____ 3,295	

*Net wages are gross wages minus federal, state, and local income tax, Social Security, and other benefits withheld from paycheck.

+440
3735

2. Giving

Church	410	+40
Other	20	
Total Giving:	$ ____ 430	

+40
470

3. Savings

Short term savings	_____	
Long term savings	_____	
Retirement savings Paula's IRA	50	<50>
Other savings ($100 w/h from Mark's paycheck)	_____	
Total Savings:	$ ____ 50	

<50>
—0—

4. Housing

Rent or mortgage	800	
Property taxes } In mortgage	_____	
Property insurance } payment	_____	
Electricity	110	
Heating/gas	_____	
Water	40	
Garbage service	_____	
Cable TV	20	<20>
Telephone	55	<20>
Cleaning	_____	
Repairs/maintenance	—0—	+80
Supplies	_____	
Improvements	50	<50>
Furnishings	_____	
Other	_____	
Total Housing:	$ ____ 1,075	

<10>
1065

Figure 4
The Robinsons' Estimated Monthly Budget Balanced
(continued)

5. Food

Groceries	$ 375	
Eating out		
School lunches	25	
Other		
Total Food:		$ 400

6. Clothing/Grooming

Purchases	70	
Cleaning	15	
Hair care	30 <20>	
Toiletries/cosmetics	15	
Total Clothing:		$ 130
		<20>
		110

7. Transportation (car payment in Debt Repayment)

Gas and oil	70	
Automobile insurance	120	
Repair and maintenance	30 +50	
Licenses/registration		
Parking and tolls		
Public transportation		
Other		
Total Transportation:		$ 220
		+50
		270

8. Medical

Doctor	10	
Dentist	10	
Prescriptions	10	
Glasses		
Health insurance ($120 per mo. w/h		
Other from paycheck)		
Total Medical:		$ 30

9. Children

School tuition	500	
Allowances	16	
School lunch		
Tutoring		
Music/dance lessons	10	
Tennis/sports	10	
Babysitting	15 <15>	
Other		
Total Children:		$ 551
		<15>
		536

Figure 4
The Robinsons' Estimated Monthly Budget Balanced
(continued)

10. Debt Repayment

    Total from Debt List (consumer debt only): $ _____ 482
                                                  +70
                                              552

11. Insurance

    Life insurance (*$480 paid annually*) $ _____ 40

    Disability _____

    Other _____

    Total Insurance: $ _____ 40

12. Recreation

    Adult allowances _____ 120 <40>

    Vacations _____ 100 <70>

    Magazines/newspapers _____ 10 <8>

    Books/tapes/records _____

    Subscriptions _____

    Hobbies _____

    Entertainment _____ 100 <50>

    Pets (vet, license) _____

    Other _____

    Total Recreation: $ _____ 330
                                        <168>

13. Gifts   162

    Christmas _____ 50 <30>

    Birthdays _____ 20 <10>

    Anniversaries _____

    Weddings/showers _____

    Graduations _____

    Office gifts _____ 10

    Other _____

    Total Gifts: $ _____ 80
                                        <40>

14. Other Personal/Business   40

    Clubs, union dues _____

    Accounting/legal   *taxes* _____ 10

    Cornerstone _____

    Other   *miscellaneous* _____ 50

    Total Other Personal/Business: $ _____ 60

    Total Spending: 3,735 $ _____ 3,878

    Net Margin/Deficit: -0- $ _____ <583>

Figure 5
Check Register

NUMBER	DATE	CHECKS ISSUED TO OR DESCRIPTION OF DEPOSIT	(-) AMOUNT OF CHECK	√T	(-) CHECK FEE	(+) AMOUNT OF DEPOSIT	BALANCE
							$ 692 47
427	9/1	TO/FOR Clark Corp. (Mark's check)	–340 00		①	+2,800 42	
	9/1	First Church (tithe)			②		
428	9/1	TO/FOR Sun Trust Bank (mortgage)	–799 87		④		
429	9/1	State Farm Insur. (Auto)	–120 14		⑦		
430	9/1	TO/FOR Florida Power and Light	–130 34		④		
431	9/1	City Water Department	–38 89		④		
432	9/2	TO/FOR Cash 231.00					
		Gasoline	–70 00		⑦		
		TO/FOR Personal allowance (adults)	–80 00		⑫		
		Dry cleaning	–15 00		⑥		
		TO/FOR Recreation	–50 00		⑫		
		Children's allowance	–16 00		⑨		
433	9/4	TO/FOR First Church (Paula's check)	–31 00		①	+ 274 62	2,076 27
	9/4	First Church (tithe)	–175 00		②		
434	9/5	TO/FOR Cash for groceries	–10 00		⑤		
435	9/10	Dr. John Smith			⑧		
436	9/10	TO/FOR Eckerd Drugs (prescription)	–10 00		⑧		
437	9/11	Dillard's (cosmetics)	–32 00		⑥		
438	9/11	TO/FOR First Christian School	–500 00		⑨		
439	9/11	First Christian School (lunch)	–13 00		⑤		
440	9/12	TO/FOR JC Penney	–48 00		⑥		
441	9/15	City Cablevision	–20 15		④		
442	9/15	TO/FOR Bell South	–38 02		④		
443	9/15	Ford Motor Credit	–263 13		⑩		
444	9/16	TO/FOR Discover	–40 00		⑩		
445	9/17	Firestone	–30 00		⑩		896 97

REMEMBER TO RECORD AUTOMATIC PAYMENTS/DEPOSITS ON DATE AUTHORIZED.

Figure 5
Check Register
(continued)

NUMBER	DATE	CHECKS ISSUED TO OR DESCRIPTION OF DEPOSIT	(-) AMOUNT OF CHECK	√T	(-) CHECK FEE	(+) AMOUNT OF DEPOSIT	BALANCE
446	9/17	TO/FOR Walmart [58.75] Recreation	-23 19		12		$ 896 97
		Housing	-35 56		4		
447	9/17	TO/FOR Citibank Visa [236.70]					
		Clothing	-92 60		6		
		TO/FOR Eating out	-52 49		12		
		Home maintenance	-31 61		4		
		TO/FOR Debt repayment	-60 00		10		
	9/18	First Church (Paula's check)			1	+ 274 62	
448	9/18	TO/FOR First Church (tithe)	-31 00		2		845 14
449	9/19	Cash for groceries	-175 00		5		
450	9/20	TO/FOR Home Depot	-32 65		4		
451	9/20	City Recreation Dept (soccer)	-55 00		9		
452	9/22	TO/FOR Smith's Amoco (auto repair)	-112 28		7		
453	9/23	Service Merchandise					
		TO/FOR (birthday gift)	-28 41		13		
454	9/25	First Christian School (lunch)	-15 00		5		
455	9/26	TO/FOR Office Depot					
		(computer supplies)	-14 33		14		
	9/27	TO/FOR Fidelity Magellan Fund (IRA)					
		(bank draft)	-50 00		3		
456	9/28	TO/FOR First National Bank					
		(education loan)	-89 00		10		$ 273 47
		TO/FOR					
		TO/FOR					

REMEMBER TO RECORD AUTOMATIC PAYMENTS/DEPOSITS ON DATE AUTHORIZED.

Figure 6

Monthly Income and Spending by Category						
For the month of _September_						
	1.	**2.**	**3.**	**4.**	**5.**	**6.**
	Income	Giving	Savings	Housing	Food	Clothing/ Grooming
Monthly Budget	3,735.00	470.00	-0-	1,065.00	400.00	110.00
Current Month Actual Income and Spending	2,800.42	340.00		799.87	175.00	15.00
	274.62	31.00		130.34	13.00	32.00
				38.89		48.00
				20.15		
				38.02		
Subtotal	3075.04	371.00	00.00	1027.27	188.00	95.00
	274.62	31.00	50.00	35.56	175.00	92.60
				31.61	15.00	
				32.65		
Total Actual	3,349.66	402.00	50.00	1,127.09	378.00	187.60

Figure 6 *(continued)*

Monthly Income and Spending

For the month of ___September___

7. Trans- portation	8. Medical	9. Children	10. Debt Repayment	11. Insurance	12. Recreation	13. Gifts	14. Other Personal
270.00	30.00	536.00	552.00	40.00	162.00	40.00	60.00
120.14	10.00	16.00	263.13		80.00		
70.00	10.00	500.00	40.00		50.00		
			30.00				
190.14	20.00	516.00	333.13	0.00	130.00	0.00	0.00
112.28		55.00	60.00		23.19	28.41	14.33
			89.00		52.49		
302.42	20.00	571.00	482.13	0.00	205.68	28.41	14.33

Figure 7
Comparison of Budgeted to Actual Income and Expenditures

As of month of September

Category	(A) Budget Amount	(B) Actual Amount	(C) (A – B) Monthly Favorable <Unfavor.>	(D) Year-to-Date Favorable <Unfavor.>
1. Income	3,735	3,350	<385>	<385>
2. Giving	470	402	68	68
3. Savings	-0-	50	<50>	<50>
4. Housing	1,065	1,127	<62>	<62>
5. Food	400	378	22	22
6. Clothing/Grooming	110	188	<78>	<78>
7. Transportation	270	302	<32>	<32>
8. Medical	30	20	10	10
9. Children	536	571	<35>	<35>
10. Debt Repayment	552	482	70	70
11. Insurance	40	-0-	40	40
12. Recreation	162	206	<44>	<44>
13. Gifts	40	28	12	12
14. Other Personal/Bus.	60	14	46	46
Total Spending	3,735	3,768	<33>	
Total Surplus <Shortfall>	-0-	<418>	<418>	

As of month of October

Category	(A) Budget Amount	(B) Actual Amount	(C) Monthly Favorable <Unfavor.>	(D) Year-to-Date Favorable <Unfavor.>
1. Income	3,735	3,624	<111>	<496>
2. Giving	470	433	37	105
3. Savings	-0-	-0-	-0-	<50>
4. Housing	1,065	1,088	<23>	<85>
5. Food	400	412	<12>	10
6. Clothing/Grooming	110	97	13	<65>
7. Transportation	270	278	<8>	<40>
8. Medical	30	32	<2>	8
9. Children	536	516	20	<15>
10. Debt Repayment	552	552	-0-	70
11. Insurance	40	-0-	40	80
12. Recreation	162	155	7	<37>
13. Gifts	40	15	25	37
14. Other Personal/Bus.	60	38	22	68
Total Spending	3,735	3,616	119	
Total Surplus <Shortfall>	-0-	8	8	

Figure 8
Check Register

NUMBER	DATE	CHECKS ISSUED TO OR DESCRIPTION OF DEPOSIT		(−) AMOUNT OF CHECK	√ T	(−) CHECK FEE	(+) AMOUNT OF DEPOSIT		BALANCE
									$ 273 47
	9/30	TO/FOR transfer to cash reserve							
		Car repairs		− 80 00		(3)		B/C/L	
		TO/FOR Home repairs/maint.		− 80 00		(3)			
		Clothing		− 70 00		(3)		B/C/L	
		TO/FOR Life insurance		− 40 00		(3)			
		Vacations		− 30 00		(3)		B/C/L	
		TO/FOR Gifts $340		− 40 00		(3)			
	9/30	TO/FOR Transfer from cash reserve						B/C/L	
		Car repairs				(3)	+ 112 00		
		TO/FOR Home repairs/maint.				(3)	+ 100 00	B/C/L	
		Clothing				(3)	+ 141 00		
		TO/FOR Gifts $381				(3)	+ 28 00	B/C/L	$ 314 47
		TO/FOR						B/C/L	
		TO/FOR							
		TO/FOR						B/C/L	
		TO/FOR							
		TO/FOR						B/C/L	
		TO/FOR							
		TO/FOR						B/C/L	
		TO/FOR							

REMEMBER TO RECORD AUTOMATIC PAYMENTS/DEPOSITS ON DATE AUTHORIZED.

Figure 9

Date	Description	SUMMARY			Cash Reserve—Irregular Expenses		
		Increase	Decrease	Balance	Car Repairs	Home Repairs/ Maint.	Clothing
	Balance forward			$1,109	309	183	48
9/30	Transfer from checking	340			80	80	70
9/30	Transfer to checking		381	1,068	<112>	<100>	<141>
	Balance			1,068	277	163	<23>

Figure 9 *(continued)*

Cash Reserve—Irregular Expenses							
Life Insurance	Vacations	Gifts				**MISCELLANEOUS**	
						Description	**Amount**
280	32	257					
40	30	40					
		<28>					
320	62	269					

Figure 10

Projected Monthly Cash Flow

Month of September

Pay dates	9/1	9/4	9/18	
Beginning cash balance	$692.47	$1,447.65	$469.99	
Cash in: paycheck	2,800.42	274.62	274.62	
dividends, interest				
Cash out:				
Gasoline	<70.00>			
Personal allowance	<80.00>			
Dry cleaning	<15.00>			
Recreation	<50.00>			
Children's allowance	<16.00>			
Groceries		<175.00>	<175.00>	
School lunch		<13.00>	<15.00>	
First Baptist (tithe)	<340.00>	<31.00>	<31.00>	
Sun Trust Bank	<799.87>			
State Farm Insurance	<120.14>			
Florida Power and Light	<130.34>			
City Water Dept.	<38.89>			
First Christian School		<500.00>		
City Cablevision		<20.15>		
Bell South		<40.00>	(estimated)	
Ford Motor Credit		<263.13>		
Discover		<40.00>		
Firestone		<30.00>		
Visa (debt repayment)		<60.00>		
Fidelity Magellan Fund			<50.00>	
First National Bank			<89.00>	
Cosmetics	<30.00>	(estimated)		
Clothes	<150.00>	(estimated)		
Soccer		<55.00>		
Car repairs	<80.00>			
Birthday gift		<25.00>	(estimated)	
Miscellaneous items	<125.00>		<125.00>	
<To> From Savings				
Ending Cash Balance	1,447.65	469.99	259.61	

Figure 11
Personal Financial Statement

Date:_____

Assets (present market value)

1. Cash/assets easily converted to cash
   a. Cash on hand and checking account $ _____
   b. Savings   _____
   c. Money market funds   _____
   d. Marketable stocks and bonds   _____
   e. Cash value of life insurance   _____
   f. Coins   _____
2. Real estate
   a. Home   _____
   b. Other real estate   _____
3. Receivables
   a. Mortgage receivables   _____
   b. Notes receivables   _____
4. Business valuation   _____
5. Personal property
   a. Automobiles   _____
   b. Furniture   _____
   c. Jewelry   _____
   d. Boat   _____
   e. Other   _____
6. Retirement
   a. IRA   _____
   b. Pension/retirement plan   _____
7. Miscellaneous   _____

Total Assets $ _____

Liabilities (current amount owed)

1. Current bills $ _____
2. Real estate
   a. Home mortgage   _____
   b. Other mortgages   _____
3. Personal debts to relatives   _____
4. Business loans   _____
5. Educational loans   _____
6. Automobile loans   _____
7. Credit cards   _____
8. Medical bills   _____
9. Life insurance loans   _____
10. Bank loans   _____
11. Installment loans   _____
12. Credit union loans   _____

Total Liabilities $ _____
Total Assets - Total Liabilities = Net Worth $ _____

Figure 12
List of Debts

Date:_____

Creditor	For What	Monthly Payment	Remaining Payments	Balance Due	Interest Rate	Scheduled Payoff Date
Totals						

Figure 13
Estimated Monthly Budget

Date:
_____

1. **Income**   **Monthly Amount**
   Wages, husband: gross _____ net* $ _____
   Wages, wife: gross _____ net* $ _____
   Dividends   _____
   Interest earned   _____
   Net rents   _____
   Net business income   _____
   Pension/retirement   _____
   Other   _____
   Total Income: $ _____

   *Net wages are gross wages minus federal, state, and local income
   tax, Social Security, and other benefits withheld from paycheck.

2. **Giving**   _____
   Church   _____
   Other $ _____
   Total Giving:

3. **Savings**   _____
   Short term savings   _____
   Long term savings   _____
   Retirement savings   _____
   Other savings
   Total Savings: $ _____

4. **Housing**
   Rent or mortgage   _____
   Property taxes   _____
   Property insurance   _____
   Electricity   _____
   Heating/gas   _____
   Water   _____
   Garbage service   _____
   Cable TV   _____
   Telephone   _____
   Cleaning   _____
   Repairs/maintenance   _____
   Supplies   _____
   Improvements   _____
   Furnishings   _____
   Other   _____
   Total Housing: $ _____

Figure 13
Estimated Monthly Budget
(continued)

5. **Food**

Groceries $_____

Eating out   _____

School lunches   _____

Other   _____

Total Food: $_____

6. **Clothing/Grooming**

Purchases   _____

Cleaning   _____

Hair care   _____

Toiletries/cosmetics   _____

Total Clothing: $_____

7. **Transportation** (car payment in Debt Repayment)

Gas and oil   _____

Automobile insurance   _____

Repair and maintenance   _____

Licenses/registration   _____

Parking and tolls   _____

Public transportation   _____

Other   _____

Total Transportation: $_____

8. **Medical**

Doctor   _____

Dentist   _____

Prescriptions   _____

Glasses   _____

Health insurance   _____

Other   _____

Total Medical: $_____

9. **Children**

School tuition   _____

Allowances   _____

School lunch   _____

Tutoring   _____

Music/dance lessons   _____

Tennis/sports   _____

Babysitting   _____

Other   _____

Total Children: $_____

Figure 13
Estimated Monthly Budget
(continued)

10. Debt Repayment

    Total from Debt List (consumer debt only): $_____

11. Insurance

    Life insurance $_____

    Disability   _____

    Other   _____

    Total Insurance: $_____

12. Recreation

    Adult allowances   _____

    Vacations   _____

    Magazines/newspapers   _____

    Books/tapes/records   _____

    Subscriptions   _____

    Hobbies   _____

    Entertainment   _____

    Pets (vet, license)   _____

    Other   _____

    Total Recreation: $_____

13. Gifts

    Christmas   _____

    Birthdays   _____

    Anniversaries   _____

    Weddings/showers   _____

    Graduations   _____

    Office gifts   _____

    Other   _____

    Total Gifts: $_____

14. Other Personal/Business

    Clubs, union dues   _____

    Accounting/legal   _____

    Cornerstone   _____

    Other   _____

    Total Other Personal/Business: $_____

    Total Spending: $_____

    Net Margin/Deficit: $_____

Figure 14

Monthly Income and Spending by Category
For the month of _____

	1. Income	2. Giving	3. Savings	4. Housing	5. Food	6. Clothing/ Grooming
Monthly Budget						
Current Month Actual Income and Spending						
Total Actual						

Figure 14 *(continued)*

Monthly Income and Spending
For the month of _____

7. Trans-portation	8. Medical	9. Children	10. Debt Repayment	11. Insurance	12. Recreation	13. Gifts	14. Other Personal

Figure 15
Comparison of Budgeted to Actual Income and Expenditures

As of month of _____

Category	(A) Budget Amount	(B) Actual Amount	(C) (A–B) Monthly Favorable <Unfavor.>	(D) Year-to- Date Favorable <Unfavor.>
1. Income				
2. Giving				
3. Savings				
4. Housing				
5. Food				
6. Clothing/Grooming				
7. Transportation				
8. Medical				
9. Children				
10. Debt Repayment				
11. Insurance				
12. Recreation				
13. Gifts				
14. Other Personal/Bus.				
Total Spending				
Total Surplus <Shortfall>				

As of month of _____

Category				
1. Income				
2. Giving				
3. Savings				
4. Housing				
5. Food				
6. Clothing/Grooming				
7. Transportation				
8. Medical				
9. Children				
10. Debt Repayment				
11. Insurance				
12. Recreation				
13. Gifts				
14. Other Personal/Bus.				
Total Spending				
Total Surplus <Shortfall>				

Figure 16

| Date | Description | SUMMARY | | | Cash Reserve—Irregular Expenses | | |
		Increase	Decrease	Balance			

Figure 16 *(continued)*

Cash Reserve—Irregular Expenses

						MISCELLANEOUS	
						Description	Amount

Figure 17

Projected Monthly Cash Flow				
Month of _____				
Pay dates				
Beginning cash balance				
Cash in:				
Cash out:				
<To> From Savings				
Ending Cash Balance				

Appendix B

Life Insurance

Life insurance is a subject most of us would avoid if we could. With our heads in the sand, we buy a small policy from our brother-in-law to get him off our backs, or pick up a policy at work without giving any thought to whether the coverage is adequate.

On the other hand, paying premiums for a policy the experts say is large enough can be a bitter pill to swallow. My health is good, and it is difficult to spend much-needed dollars to cover the possibility of dying. But I know I must do it for my family's sake. I have heard too many stories of widows struggling to raise their children to kid myself about the importance of adequate life insurance.

The question is, How much is enough? A rough rule of thumb is ten to twelve times the insured person's annual income. (My insurance agent tells me this is way too simplistic, but I think it's a good guide and has the advantage of being a simple calculation.) Although Elizabeth is not employed outside of the home, I have a policy on her life because of the cost of employing someone to do all the work she handles at home. I know I could never singlehandedly raise two teenagers and run the household while teaching and managing a business.

Understand the types of insurance before deciding what to buy. There are two basic types: term and cash value. Term is pure death benefit, and cash value combines a death benefit and an investment portion.

Term insurance can be sold as annual renewable term, level term, or decreasing term. *Annual renewable term insurance* allows someone to buy a policy for a specific amount of death benefit at a set annual premium and renew it by continuing to pay an increasing annual premium. Years later the increases make the policy unaffordable. Ideally at this point the children will be educated, the debts paid off, and money accumulated for retirement, so the need for insurance will be greatly diminished. *Level term insurance* allows someone to buy a policy for a specific amount of death benefit and pay a set annual premium for ten, fifteen, or twenty years, after which the annual premium goes up substantially. *Decreasing term insurance* is a policy with a death benefit that decreases over a set period. It is usually sold through lenders to pay off the remaining balance on home mortgages or auto loans if the insured person dies. I have never found this type of policy a good buy and don't recommend it.

Cash value insurance can be sold as whole life, universal life, and variable life. *Whole life insurance policies* have been around for years and are rarely sold anymore because better policies have been developed. For the investment portion of the policy, returns are usually quite low because the funds historically were invested conservatively. Also, administrative and marketing costs in the policy are high, leaving a much smaller portion of the premium dollar available for the investment portion. *Universal life* and *variable life policies* can have attractive projected investment returns. Tax laws also permit insurance agents to recommend strategies for accessing funds unavailable with other types of investing. There is usually tremendous flexibility in the premium dollar paid over time, the amount of insurance death benefit obtained, and the amount put into the investment portion.

Rather than get into the well-known debate over which type of insurance is better, we recommend to all of our clients that they obtain the most affordable term insurance from a top-rated insurance company and get an adequate death benefit. Whether insurance is also a good investment vehicle is beyond the scope of this book.

At this writing, level term insurance products seem to give the best value for the premium dollar spent. Shop around. Premiums for comparable policies from different top-rated companies can vary by a large margin. For more information on competitive products, you could contact Select Quote at 800-343-1985. The service will give quotes over the phone and send you a comparison from five companies.

Appendix C

Projecting Cash Needs for the Month

A monthly cash flow projection (fig. 17 in appendix A) can be helpful if things are extremely tight or if your income is irregular. Do one at the start of every month. Figure 10 in appendix A shows a projection of monthly cash flow for the Robinsons. The first number at the top of the first column is the actual cash balance from the checkbook register, $692.47 (see fig. 5). Entries in three columns represent three times in the month when the Robinsons receive income: once from Mark's paycheck (9/1) and twice from Paula's paycheck (9/4 and 9/18).

The purpose of the cash projection is to determine the estimated monthly cash needs and make sure there will be enough money to cover them in the checking account. All anticipated payments and dates are shown. In the first column, starting with the beginning cash balance, cash in from paycheck is added, and all payments are subtracted, as shown by the symbol < >. The total labeled Ending Cash Balance is at the bottom of the column. This number, $1,447.65, also is recorded at the top of the next column as the beginning balance for that cycle, and so on across the schedule.

Look at the lines for Bell South and Birthday Gift. To the right of both numbers, "(estimated)" has been written in because we don't have the bills, and we don't know what these amounts will be. A line labeled Miscellaneous Items covers other smaller unpredictable cash needs that will come up during the month.

Sometimes payments that must be made exceed the money in the checking account. Either money has to be moved from savings to checking to cover the shortfall, or some things will have to be postponed. This is the real benefit of the schedule, allowing us to determine how we will handle this circumstance before a serious problem develops.

The last line right above Ending Cash Balance is labeled <To> From Savings. When money is transferred between savings and checking, it is shown on this line. If I have more money in the checking account than needed to cover the monthly payments, I will transfer the surplus to savings to avoid the temptation to spend it. The transfer is shown with < > because the funds are being removed from the checking account. In other months when I need additional funds to cover payments, I will do the reverse and transfer money from savings to checking.

The Projected Monthly Cash Flow schedule gives me peace of mind. I tend to get anxious about our checking account when I don't know where it stands for the next few weeks. (I know it is a sin to be anxious, but an organized approach to finances helps me avoid this sin.) Our income fluctuates considerably, and this schedule allows me to project for several months to anticipate cash shortfalls. I know if I'll have to move funds into checking from other places besides savings, or if I need to be praying because of cash needs beyond our immediately available resources.

Once you get comfortable with using this schedule, it should take about ten to fifteen minutes to prepare it each month.

Appendix D
Wisdom from the Bible

DEBT

Proverbs 22:7: "The rich rule over the poor, and the borrower is servant to the lender."

Psalm 37:21: "The wicked borrow and do not repay, but the righteous give generously."

DESIRES OF OUR HEART

Psalm 37:4–7: "Delight yourself in the LORD and he will give you the desires of your heart. Commit your way to the LORD; trust in him and he will do this: He will make your righteousness shine like the dawn, the justice of your cause like the noonday sun. Be still before the LORD and wait patiently for him; do not fret when men succeed in their ways, when they carry out their wicked schemes."

DESPAIR

Psalm 13: "How long, O LORD? Will you forget me forever? How long will you hide your face from me? How long must I wrestle with my thoughts and every day have sorrow in my heart? How long will my enemy triumph over me? Look on me and answer, O LORD my God. Give light to my eyes, or I will sleep in death; my enemy will say, 'I have overcome him,' and my foes will rejoice when I fall. But I trust in your unfailing love;

my heart rejoices in your salvation. I will sing to the LORD, for
he has been good to me."

Psalm 42:5: "Why are you downcast, O my soul? Why so disturbed
within me? Put your hope in God, for I will yet praise him, my
Savior and my God."

EMERGENCY RESERVE

Proverbs 22:3: "A prudent man sees danger and takes refuge, but
the simple keep going and suffer for it."

The Living Bible: "A prudent man foresees the difficulties ahead
and prepares for them; the simpleton goes blindly on and suf-
fers the consequences."

FEAR

Psalm 46:1–2: "God is our refuge and strength, an ever-present
help in trouble. Therefore we will not fear, though the earth
give way and the mountains fall into the heart of the sea."

GOD FIRST

Haggai 1:2–13: "This is what the LORD Almighty says: 'These
people say, "The time has not yet come for the LORD's house to
be built."' Then the word of the LORD came through the prophet
Haggai: 'Is it a time for you yourselves to be living in your pan-
eled houses, while this house remains a ruin?' Now this is what
the LORD Almighty says: 'Give careful thought to your ways.
You have planted much, but have harvested little. You eat, but
never have enough. You drink, but never have your fill. You put
on clothes, but are not warm. You earn wages, only to put them
in a purse with holes in it.' This is what the LORD Almighty says:
'Give careful thought to your ways. Go up into the mountains
and bring down timber and build the house, so that I may take
pleasure in it and be honored,' says the LORD. 'You expected
much, but see, it turned out to be little. What you brought home,

I blew away. Why?' declares the LORD Almighty. 'Because of my house, which remains a ruin, while each of you is busy with his own house. Therefore, because of you the heavens have withheld their dew and the earth its crops. I called for a drought on the fields and the mountains, on the grain, the new wine, the oil and whatever the ground produces, on men and cattle, and on the labor of your hands.' Then Zerubbabel son of Shealtiel, Joshua son of Jehozadak, the high priest, and the whole remnant of the people obeyed the voice of the LORD their God and the message of the prophet Haggai, because the LORD their God had sent him. And the people feared the LORD. Then Haggai, the LORD's messenger, gave this message of the LORD to the people: 'I am with you,' declares the LORD."

GOD IS IN CONTROL

Ecclesiastes 7:14: "When times are good, be happy; but when times are bad, consider: God has made the one as well as the other. Therefore, a man cannot discover anything about his future."

The Living Bible: "Enjoy prosperity whenever you can, and when hard times strike, realize that God gives one as well as the other—so that everyone will realize that nothing is certain in this life."

GOD'S WILL

Psalm 25:12–14: "Who, then, is the man that fears the LORD? He will instruct him in the way chosen for him. He will spend his days in prosperity, and his descendants will inherit the land. The LORD confides in those who fear him; he makes his covenant known to them."

HOPE IN GOD

Psalm 42:5: "Why are you downcast, O my soul? Why so disturbed within me? Put your hope in God, for I will yet praise him, my Savior and my God."

Joy

1 Thessalonians 5:16–18: "Be joyful always; pray continually; give thanks in all circumstances, for this is God's will for you in Christ Jesus."

Know Your Financial Condition

Proverbs 27:23–24: "Be sure you know the condition of your flocks, give careful attention to your herds; for riches do not endure forever, and a crown is not secure for all generations."

The Living Bible: "Riches can disappear fast. And the king's crown doesn't stay in his family forever—so watch your business interests closely. Know the state of your flocks and your herds."

Luke 14:28–30: "Suppose one of you wants to build a tower. Will he not first sit down and estimate the cost to see if he has enough money to complete it? For if he lays the foundation and is not able to finish it, everyone who sees it will ridicule him, saying, 'This fellow began to build and was not able to finish.'"

Proverbs 14:8: "The wisdom of the prudent is to give thought to their ways, but the folly of fools is deception."

The Living Bible: "The wise man looks ahead. The fool attempts to fool himself and won't face facts."

Long-Term Perspective

Proverbs 21:5: "The plans of the diligent lead to profit as surely as haste leads to poverty."

The Living Bible: "Steady plodding brings prosperity; hasty speculation brings poverty."

Needs Met

Matthew 6:25–34: "Therefore I tell you, do not worry about your life, what you will eat or drink; or about your body, what you will wear. Is not life more important than food, and the body more important than clothes? Look at the birds of the air; they do not sow or reap or store away in barns, and yet your heavenly Father feeds them. Are you not much more valuable than they? Who of you by worrying can add a single hour to his life? And why do you worry about clothes? See how the lilies of the field grow. They do not labor or spin. Yet I tell you that not even Solomon in all his splendor was dressed like one of these. If that is how God clothes the grass of the field, which is here today and tomorrow is thrown into the fire, will he not much more clothe you, O you of little faith? So do not worry, saying, 'What shall we eat?' or 'What shall we drink?' or 'What shall we wear?' For the pagans run after all these things, and your heavenly Father knows that you need them. But seek first his kingdom and his righteousness, and all these things will be given to you as well. Therefore do not worry about tomorrow, for tomorrow will worry about itself. Each day has enough trouble of its own."

PATIENCE

Psalm 37:7, 34: "Be still before the LORD and wait patiently for him; do not fret when men succeed in their ways, when they carry out their wicked schemes. Wait for the LORD and keep his way. He will exalt you to inherit the land; when the wicked are cut off, you will see it."

PLANNING

Proverbs 14:8: "The wisdom of the prudent is to give thought to their ways, but the folly of fools is deception."

The Living Bible: "The wise man looks ahead. The fool attempts to fool himself and won't face facts."

Proverbs 16:9: "In his heart a man plans his course, but the LORD determines his steps."

The Living Bible: "We should make plans—counting on God to direct us."

Proverbs 16:1: "To man belong the plans of the heart, but from the LORD comes the reply of the tongue."

The Living Bible: "We can make our plans, but the final outcome is in God's hands."

Proverbs 22:3: "A prudent man sees danger and takes refuge, but the simple keep going and suffer for it."

Isaiah 32:8: "The noble man makes noble plans, and by noble deeds he stands."

Isaiah 8:10: "Devise your strategy, but it will be thwarted; propose your plan, but it will not stand, for God is with us."

PRAY

1 Thessalonians 5:16–18: "Be joyful always; pray continually; give thanks in all circumstances, for this is God's will for you in Christ Jesus."

PROSPERITY

Psalm 1:1–3: "Blessed is the man who does not walk in the counsel of the wicked or stand in the way of sinners or sit in the seat of mockers. But his delight is in the law of the LORD, and on his law he meditates day and night. He is like a tree planted by streams of water, which yields its fruit in season and whose leaf does not wither. Whatever he does prospers."

Proverbs 21:5: "The plans of the diligent lead to profit as surely as haste leads to poverty."

The Living Bible: "Steady plodding brings prosperity; hasty speculation brings poverty."

QUIET AND SIMPLE LIFE

1 Thessalonians 4:11–12: "Make it your ambition to lead a quiet life, to mind your own business and to work with your hands, just as we told you, so that your daily life may win the respect of outsiders and so that you will not be dependent on anybody."

REPAYING LOANS

Psalm 37:21: "The wicked borrow and do not repay, but the righteous give generously."

SAVING

Proverbs 21:20: "In the house of the wise are stores of choice food and oil, but a foolish man devours all he has."
The Living Bible: "The wise man saves for the future, but the foolish man spends whatever he gets."
Proverbs 6:6–8: "Go to the ant, you sluggard; consider its ways and be wise! It has no commander, no overseer or ruler, yet it stores its provisions in summer and gathers its food at harvest."
The Living Bible: "Take a lesson from the ants, you lazy fellow. Learn from their ways and be wise! For though they have no king to make them work, yet they labor hard all summer, gathering food for the winter."

SEEKING GOD'S WILL

Psalm 37:4: "Delight yourself in the LORD and he will give you the desires of your heart."

SEEKING RICHES

Proverbs 23:4–5: "Do not wear yourself out to get rich; have the wisdom to show restraint. Cast but a glance at riches, and they are gone, for they will surely sprout wings and fly off to the sky like an eagle."

STEWARDSHIP (Managing Another's Resources)

1 Chronicles 29:11–12, 14: "For everything in heaven and earth is yours. Yours, O LORD, is the kingdom; you are exalted as head over all. Wealth and honor come from you; you are the ruler of

all things. In your hands are strength and power to exalt and give strength to all. Everything comes from you, and we have given you only what comes from your hand."

TRIALS

James 1:2–6: "Consider it pure joy, my brothers, whenever you face trials of many kinds, because you know that the testing of your faith develops perseverance. Perseverance must finish its work so that you may be mature and complete, not lacking anything. If any of you lacks wisdom, he should ask God, who gives generously to all without finding fault, and it will be given to him. But when he asks, he must believe and not doubt, because he who doubts is like a wave of the sea, blown and tossed by the wind."

TRUST IN GOD

2 Samuel 22:31: "As for God, his way is perfect; the word of the LORD is flawless. He is a shield for all who take refuge in him."

Psalm 5:11: "But let all who take refuge in you be glad; let them ever sing for joy. Spread your protection over them, that those who love your name may rejoice in you."

Psalm 7:1: "O LORD my God, I take refuge in you; save and deliver me from all who pursue me."

Psalm 40:4: "Blessed is the man who makes the LORD his trust."

Psalm 9:9–10: "The LORD is a refuge for the oppressed, a stronghold in times of trouble. Those who know your name will trust in you, for you, LORD, have never forsaken those who seek you."

Psalm 18:30: "As for God, his way is perfect; the word of the LORD is flawless. He is a shield for all who take refuge in him."

Psalm 32:10: "Many are the woes of the wicked, but the LORD's unfailing love surrounds the man who trusts in him."

Psalm 84:5, 12: "Blessed are those whose strength is in you. O LORD Almighty, blessed is the man who trusts in you."

Proverbs 3:5–6, 24–26: "Trust in the LORD with all your heart and lean not on your own understanding; in all your ways acknowledge him, and he will make your paths straight. When you lie down, you will not be afraid; when you lie down, your sleep will be sweet. Have no fear of sudden disaster or of the ruin that overtakes the wicked, for the LORD will be your confidence and will keep your foot from being snared."

WISDOM

James 1:5: "If any of you lacks wisdom, he should ask God, who gives generously to all without finding fault, and it will be given to him."

WITHOUT ERROR (THE BIBLE)

Psalm 18:30: "As for God, his way is perfect; the word of the LORD is flawless. He is a shield for all who take refuge in him."

WORRY

Matthew 6:25–34: "Therefore I tell you, do not worry about your life, what you will eat or drink; or about your body, what you will wear. Is not life more important than food, and the body more important than clothes? Look at the birds of the air; they do not sow or reap or store away in barns, and yet your heavenly Father feeds them. Are you not much more valuable than they? Who of you by worrying can add a single hour to his life? And why do you worry about clothes? See how the lilies of the field grow. They do not labor or spin. Yet I tell you that not even Solomon in all his splendor was dressed like one of these. If that is how God clothes the grass of the field, which is here today and tomorrow is thrown into the fire, will he not much more clothe you, O you of little faith? So do not worry, saying, 'What shall we eat?' or 'What shall we drink?' or 'What shall we wear?' For the pagans run after all these things, and your heavenly Father knows that you need them. But seek first his kingdom and his righteousness, and all these things will be given to you as well. Therefore do not worry about tomorrow, for tomorrow will worry about itself. Each day has enough trouble of its own."

Appendix E

Resources

PAYING OFF YOUR MORTGAGE EARLY

The Banker's Secret, a book by Marc Eisenson, provides ideas for developing a strategy to pay off your mortgage early. Software for the calculations and a quarterly newsletter that focuses on living on less also are available. For information write or call:

The Banker's Secret
Box 78
Elizaville, NY 12523
800-255-0899

INVESTING WISELY

Charles Schwab and Company, discount stockbrokers. Provides source for stocks, bonds, money market funds, and mutual funds. Call:
800-435-4000

Austin Pryor, publisher of *Sound Mind Investing* newsletter. Christian-based investment advice for middle-income households. Twelve issues per year, $59. For a free sample newsletter, write:

SMI
Post Office Box 22128
Louisville, KY 40252-0128
502-426-7420

Ronald Blue and Company is a firm of registered investment advisors. Christian-based guidance and fee-only investment management is available for investing twenty-five thousand dollars and up.
Ronald Blue and Company
1100 Johnson Ferry Road, N.E., Suite 600
Atlanta, GA 30342
404-255-0147

COST OF COLLEGE

Peterson's Guide to Four-Year Colleges annually publishes information on majors, admissions requirements, cost, financial aid, and campus life at more than two thousand colleges in the United States and Canada. The guide is available in any full-service bookstore.

CAREER GUIDANCE

Career Pathways offers an assessment for determining a fulfilling career path based on your personality, interests, and abilities. Career Pathways is affiliated with:
Money Matters
P.O. Box 100
Gainesville, GA 30503
800-722-1976

Maximum Potential offers an assessment for helping individuals discover how God has uniquely equipped them for work. Maximum Potential is a nonprofit Christian career development and transition ministry and can be reached at:
P. O. Box 24618
Tempe, AZ 85285-4618
602-756-0164

LIFE INSURANCE

Select Quote will give you quotes on life insurance over the telephone and send out a comparison of five policies. Call:
800-343-1985

James D. Dean, CPA, is director of associate development for Cornerstone Management Associates, and he is chief executive officer and cofounder of the Institute for Debt Free Living. He is also on the faculty at Nova Southeastern University, teaching accounting and finance. He was formerly controller for Coral Ridge Ministries and director of the Management Development Center at Jacksonville State University.

Charles W. Morris is president of the Philadelphia Marketing Group, which assists numerous companies and non-profits with communication and planning and also assists Christian organizations with fundraising. He is a former bureau chief with United Press International and press secretary for two former U.S. senators. He serves as an elder in his church in Colorado.